Motorbooks International Illustrated Buyer's Guide Series

Illustrated

MICRO & MINI CAR

BUYER'S ★ GUIDE™

Bill Siuru

Dedication
To my Dad who I thank, or blame,
for my life long passion for cars of all types and sizes.

First published in 1995 by Motorbooks
International Publishers & Wholesalers,
729 Prospect Avenue, PO Box1, Osceola, WI
54020 USA

© William D. Siuru, 1995

Motorbooks International books are also
available at discounts in bulk quantity for
industrial or sales-promotional use. For details
write to Special Sales Manager at the Publisher's
address

Library of Congress Cataloging-in-Publication
Data
Siuru, William D.
    Illustrated micro and mini car buyer's guide/
    Bill Siuru.
    p. cm.—(Motorbooks International illustrated
    buyer's guide series)
    Includes index.
    ISBN 0-7603-0070-4 (pbk.)
1. Compact cars—History. I. Title. II. Series.
TL15.S53   1995
629.222—dc20   95-392

On the front cover: A pair of beautiful minicars.
On the left is a 1962 Morris Mini-Cooper S owned
by Myk Sitkin of Burbank, California. The 1959
BMW Isetta 300 is owned by Marilyn Felling of
Topanga Canyon, California.

On the back cover: A row of Messerschmitt
Kabinenrollers. The driver and passenger sat in
tandem under a plexiglass bubble dome.

Printed and bound in the United States of America

Contents

Acknowledgments

I thank a large number of minicar and micro-car enthusiasts who supplied information, brochures, and photographs and reviewed the various sections on particular marques for completeness and accuracy. I hope I have included all those who helped. My sincerest apologies to anyone I might have missed.

Chris Alford Racing and Sportscars, Alpine
Bob Allan, Imp
Jean Allan, Crosley
David Allen, Citroen
Michael Antonich, Fiat Jolly
Charles Armstrong-Wilson, Fairthorpe
Rich Bachmann, Panhard and Vespa
Michael Bainter, Crosley
Brian Baker, Honda
Paul J. Bates, ISO Isetta
Bill Becker, Fiat
John Bennet, Heinkel and Trojan
Tony Bond, Panhard
Lee Bortmas, Bantam Jeep
Stephen Boyd, Scootacar
Byron W. Brill, Auto Union and DKW
Roger Bryson, Ginetta
Roy M. R. Bunker, Goggomobil and Glas
Chris Clay, Clan
Alan Coffland, Citroen 2CV
Jim Conner, Austin American and Bantam
Jim Craig, DKW
Herbert W. Deeks, Citroen
Paul and Edwina DeRousse, BMW 700
Doug Dexter, Austin 7
Ronald Eppley, Renault

Marilyn J. Felling, Isetta
Ernest Freestone, King Midget
Beau Gabel, Turner
John Gerber, Heinkel
Rev. A. J. Goldberger, Crosley
Gerron S. Hite, Berkeley
James L. Hockenhull, Crosley
Otto Hoffmann, DKW
Wolfgang Hoffmann, Citroen 2CV
Bill Hossfield, Eshelman and King Mitchell
Helmut Hubener, Goliath
Lea Hyke, Isetta
John Jensen, Isetta
Gordon Jolley, Turner
Dr. Manfred Kloppmann, Zundapp
Marianne Kunnecke, Automuseum Story
Chika Kurakawa, Mazda
Jean-Yves Lardinois, Alpine and Deutsch-Bonnet
Fred Lieb, Turner
W. Conway Link, Heinkel
Syd LeSueur, American Bantam
John E. Lloyd, Lloyd
Richard Maszy, Subaru 360
Dave Major, Isetta
A. Meyer, DKW, Isetta, and Citroen
Doug Milota, British Fords
Ronald and Lillian J. Mitchell, American Austin and Bantam
Roger Morris, Standard
Tom J. Nara, Bond
Mark Norris III, various minicars
Hubert H. Onstad, Fiat Jolly
Chris Obert, Fiat

Ed Parsil, Subaru 360
John D. Patton, Renault
Joe Pendergast, Historic Sportscar Racing, Ltd.
Joe Perry, Ginetta
Daniel Pflug, Martin
Neil Phalen, Austin 7
David Pilpan-Augustyn, Imp
Steve Piantieri, Fiat Jolly
John Rawlins, Davrian
George Regalo, Rosetta Cabrio
M. L. Rodgers, Bantam Jeep
Steve Rossi, Saab
Rodger Sawicki, BMW 600
Dave Scott, Fairthorpe
Mike Self, Fiat and Renault
Dave Sharp, Trabant
Barney Sharratt, Austin A30/A35
Dick Strange, Daihatsu
Jim Sykes, NSU
Jeffrey M. Trepel, Hino
Sean Vigle, various minicars
Merkel Weiss, Abarth, Fiat, and Moretti
John Weitlauf, King Midget
Billy Wells, Toyota
Janet Westcott, Fiat
Paul Wigton, DKW
Tim Winker, Saab
Kazmier Wysocki, DAF, Frisky, and Goggomobil

Also greatly appreciated is the help provided by the staffs in the public relations offices at the various companies and organizations who took the time to go through their files to find photos and information that was most useful in putting this book together.

Audi AG
Austin Rover
Automuseum Story GmbH
BMW AG and BMW NA
S. A. Andre Citroen
Daihatsu Motor Company, Ltd.
Fiat
Ford Motor Company, Ltd. (Dagenham)
Garratt Antique Auto Collection
Harrah's Automobile Collection
Honda Motor Company, Ltd.
Hyman Limited Classic Cars
Japanese Automobile Manufacturers Association, Inc.
Marcos Sales, Ltd.
Mazda Motor Corporation
Midas Cars, Ltd.
The Museum of Automobiles, Morrilton, Arkansas
Nissan Motor Company, Ltd.
Ogle Design, Ltd.
Reliant Motors, Ltd.
Regie Nationale de Usines Renault
Saab-Scania and Saab Cars USA
SEAT
Speedwell Performance Conversions, Ltd.
Subaru (Fuji Heavy Industries)
Suzuki Motor Company
Toyota Motor Corporation

Introduction

To most car enthusiasts, collectable cars mean vintage sports cars, foreign exotics, muscle cars, or classic luxury cars. At the bottom of their lists are cars whose original purpose was just to provide minimal, low-cost transportation. Fortunately, there is a growing group of enthusiasts who are giving microcars and minicars their due respect and having fun doing it.

Collecting minicars and microcars can become an addiction. They do not take up much room, several can be stored in a normal two-car garage, and most can be purchased for a "song." Dedicated collectors of these tiny cars often own several to many, covering a variety of marques. Like cute puppies, collectors find it hard to pass up an abandoned minicar or microcar.

Most minicar and microcar collectors do not take their hobby as seriously as do collectors of larger cars. Perhaps it is because their cars have been the butt of many a joke and are often greeted with "cute" remarks when they drive their tiny cars.

What is a Minicar or Microcar?

Defining what is a minicar or microcar depends on who is doing the defining. For this *Illustrated Buyer's Guide*, the line is drawn more or less at 1000cc (1ltr) engine displacement. In some cases, cars with larger displacements are included because they started out small and grew. As to the difference between microcar and minicar, generally micro is smaller than mini, but the dividing line is fuzzy.

There are far too many vehicles that fit the definition to be included between the pages of a single Buyer's Guide. For instance, in the early days, cycle cars were very popular, especially in England and on the Continent. These are not included. Then there are the many current minicars sold in Japan, as well as the 1ltr cars included in European auto makers' catalogs. Even in the United States, it is still possible to buy a new Geo Metro with a three-cylinder, 1ltr engine. While these will be touched upon, they are really used cars and not usually of particular interest to collectors.

Then there are the huge number of one-offs that never reached serious production. Some were prototypes and concept cars. Others were ideas, often rather off-the-wall designs, tried by specialty car builders, entrepreneurial would-be auto makers, or even individuals who built them in their garages. These will usually not be included. Also excluded are cars that are powered by other than internal-combustion engines. Electric, solar, spring, or pedal-powered cars are not too exciting to most car collectors.

Buying a Microcar or Minicar

Buying a microcar or minicar usually involves more emotion than rational car buying. Like their size, their values, with very few exceptions, will always remain small. If you want a collector car with substantial investment potential, look elsewhere. Minicars and microcars should be bought "just for the fun of it." Likewise, investments in major restorations will probably never pay back. It can be almost as expensive to restore a Jaguar as an Austin A30. While you might not want to use a Messerschmitt or Isetta for everyday transport, most of these cars were originally built to provide basic transportation, though perhaps not at interstate speeds. Indeed, Renault Dauphines, Fiat 600s, two-cycle Saabs, and DKWs were seriously marketed in the United States for commuter duty and did a reasonable-to-excellent job. My Fiat 600 was a great commuter car, as were the Renault 4CV, Goliath, and NSU Prinz used by friends in Southern California in the 1960s.

The more venturous even made long distance trips, such as one Boston college professor who took his whole family on a summer sabbatical to Colorado in a Citroen Deux Chevaux/(2CV). Or how about the college students who drove an Isetta from California to do some skiing in Utah? Almost every minicar and microcar was designed for economical, reliable transportation. That's more than you can say for some Ferraris, Lamborghinis, or other megabuck supercars.

Speaking of daily drivers, many of the later models that were not sold in the United States cannot now be brought in and registered here, because they do not meet safety and emission standards. For example, Citroen 2CVs are now imported into the United States, but these are "restored" or "remanufactured" pre-1968 models, making them exempt from these regulations. In some states, it is becoming difficult to get two-stroke engines like those used in Saabs and DKWs registered because of emission regulations.

While minicars might be cheap to buy, they sometimes are quite expensive to restore. This is especially true of the more esoteric models where replacement parts no longer exist and, therefore, require expensive machine work to duplicate. Microcar and minicar owners are great "make-doers." They can keep cars running by substituting parts from other marques and sometimes motorcycles. Frequently, you will find some pretty creative substitutions like Berkeleys with Honda motorcycle engines or Morris Minors with Nissan engines. Sometimes it's done because the original powerplant is not available or it's too expensive. Other times it is done because the owner wants to go faster or

Minicar and microcar shows are popping up around the country as interest in this segment of the collectable car hobby grows in popularity. *Bill Siuru*

desires greater reliability and durability.

This creativity extends to trim, instruments, wheels, bumpers, and just about everything else. This can drive collectors who are sticklers for authenticity wild. Having "all the numbers match" is of little concern to most minicar and microcar fans. Adding to the authenticity problem is the fact that many of the small manufacturers assembled cars from whatever parts were currently available in the Fiat, Renault, or BMC parts bin. Compounding the difficulty, manufacturers with creditors knocking on the door put more priority on meeting the payroll than keeping records.

These cars were mostly built by auto makers who often cut corners to cut costs. They were also designed to last a few years, not forever. Because they were cheap to buy, many owners did not have the money or interest for routine maintenance. They were used, abused, and then abandoned. Cars brought to the United States were driven under conditions, such as long distances at high speeds, for which they were not designed. All this added up to disaster, not the least of which are huge amounts of rust in cars in the salt belt. And do not be lulled into a false sense of security because there is a fiberglass body. Underneath there are metal components that can and do rust.

Investment Rating

There are several factors that influence the investment potential of a collectable car—design, performance, innovation and engineering, historic importance, build quality and luxury, and rarity.

While beauty is in the eye of the beholder, with a few notable exceptions, most microcars and minicars have looks that "only an owner can love." The exceptions are the special-bodied cars, and in some cases, production cars like the BMW 700, Renault Caravelle, and NSU Wankel Spider. Italian carrozzerias such as Bertone, Ghia, Micholetti, Pininfarina, and Zagato did build some interesting, if not beautiful, cars around the smallish mechanics. These designers are to be especially heralded because it is much harder to package a small car than a large car without producing a funky look. Some of these special-bodied cars have bright investment potential and are worthy of a top-notch "professional" restoration. Plan on using an experienced, read "expensive," panel beater to get things right.

Most of these tiny cars sacrificed mphs for mpgs. However, there are many decent performers, especially in the handling department. Cars with hyphenated names that include Abarth, Gordini, Martini, OSCA, or Coventry-Climax are the most fun, and consequently make good investments. Alpines, Berkeleys, Crosley Hot Shots, Deutsch-Bonnets, Honda S600/S800s, and Turners are good to great sports cars.

Innovation is one area where microcars really shine. In no other segment of the automotive world will you find the likes of an Isetta or Heinkel bubble car, two-stroke DKWs and Saabs, a "which way is it going?" Zundapp Janus 250, or three-wheel Bonds and Reliants. Just about every concept and configuration was tried. Some worked; many did not. Considering the lowest possible cost goal for most designers, the engineering was far from sophisticated. Many could be engineered a bit better.

There are many microcars and minicars of historical importance. BMW got its start in the minicar business and survived in the lean postwar days with cars like the Isetta and BMW 700. Felix Wankel's rotary engine made its debut in a minicar. Alec Issigonis' Minis pioneered the front-wheel drive/transverse engine layout that would be copied by almost all major auto makers.

Then there are the sports cars with a racing history. Any car described by an "ex-XXXX" indicating it was driven by a noted race car driver, is usually a great investment. Today, many very small sports cars are popular in vintage racing, where to many participants driving something very different is more important than going fast.

Luxury and microcars or minicars is really an oxymoron. If you want limousine luxury, a host of creature comforts, and a land-yacht ride, you are probably not a minicar or microcar type. Build quality is not the strong suit of a class of cars aimed mostly at those with very limited budgets. Some were downright crude. Most were just so-so. Very few, if any, can be called exquisite.

When it comes to one-to-five star ratings, it is important to note that these are relative to other minicars and microcars. A five-star Isetta Cabriolet or Mini-Cooper S is not equivalent to a five-star Aston Martin or Rolls-Royce, and never will be.

Star Ratings:

★ Mass-produced sedans, station wagons, and vans that are only a few years old and are just used cars and probably always will be just used cars.

★★ More limited editions of later mass-produced models with improved performance options or more desirable body styles such as coupes. Older models available in large numbers with entry-level powerplants and trim in less desirable four-door sedan or station wagon form.

★★★ Popular vintage minicars and microcars with upscale powerplants and trim. Two-door sedans, coupes, and four-doors with, for example, sun roofs. Cars made in large numbers.

★★★★ Cars with an important history such as the first series of a long-running and popular series. Open-top convertibles and roadsters built on platforms used by more mundane models. Sporty cars, but not sports cars.

★★★★★ Rare edition models with high-performance modifications done by a renowned "tuner" or with handsome, custom coachwork done by a renowned coachbuilder. Competition cars with a famous and documented racing history. True sports cars with spectacular performance, at least for their size.

For those who want something really rare and unusual, how about a German-built 1954 Kleinschnittger F125? These tiny, open two-seaters were built between 1950 and 1957 and were powered by a single-cylinder, two-stroke, 125cc, Ilo engine up front. *Automuseum Story*

Chapter 1

United States

Virtually all the factors that favored mini-cars and microcars in other parts of the world were absent in the United States. Unlike Europe and Japan, United States gasoline was abundant and cheap—twenty-five cents a gallon or less. There was no real incentive to sacrifice luxury and performance by buying a car that got 30, 40, or 50mpg. License fees and road taxes in most states have been kept low compared to the high, even confiscatory, taxes found in Europe and Japan. Unlike Europe, taxes and fees are either based on vehicle weight or value, not usually on engine horsepower or displacement. Thus taxes were not a factor in making a buying decision.

This 1933 American Austin roadster, designed by Count Alexis deSakhnoffsky, can only be described as "cute." *Harrah's Automobile Collection*

It costs almost as much to build a small car as a larger one. When the American Austin was introduced in 1930, it cost $445, about $5 more than a 1930 Ford Model A phaeton. Likewise, a 1947 Crosley started at around $900. For about $300, you could buy a base Chevrolet or Ford. While these were rather spartan, so was the Crosley.

Then there are American driving conditions with long distances between destinations. Minicars like the American Austin and Bantam, Crosley, and King Midget were pretty much city cars.

American minicars were brought out during the times they had the best chance for success. The American Austin appeared during the Depression. However, Americans still preferred a big, used car rather than a small, new one. In the 1930s, good used cars could be bought for a few hundred dollars, and basic transportation could be purchased for as little as $10 or $20. The Crosley and King Midget did reasonably well immediately after World War II, when anything with wheels sold. But as supplies of conventional American cars became abundant, the demand for Crosleys, and to a lesser extent King Midgets, dropped off drastically.

American Austin and American Bantam

The American Austin and Bantam story starts in Britain with the Austin

Seven designed by Herbert Austin. The Austin Seven made its public debut in 1922 and was an instant success. Confident with this success, Austin sailed, in early 1929, with four Austin Sevens to conquer new markets in the United States. Austin settled on Butler, Pennsylvania, to set up production, because it had a waiting and able work force, and it was close to the East Coast, so bringing in British components would be relatively easy. Support in the form of about $450,000 from the Butler business community helped cinch the deal.

1930-36 American Austin

The American Austin was similar to its English sibling mechanically, except that engine parts were mostly not interchangeable. The location of starters, generators, carburetors, and so on were swapped from one side to the other. Electric components came from Auto-Lite versus Britain's Lucas.

There was a 75in wheelbase and an overall length of under 10ft. The front suspension used a traverse leaf spring, and the rear had quarter-elliptic springs. Four-wheel mechanical brakes were used. Power came from a 13hp at 3300rpm, 745cc (45.6cid), four-cylinder engine, sufficient for a car that, depending on the body style, weighed 1,035 to 1,300lb.

The car was quality-built. For instance, the engine, with a 5:1 compression ratio, used ball and roller bearings, and each engine was tested on a dynamometer before it was installed. The car's top speed was a leisurely 50mph, and maybe 55mph with a tailwind.

Considering the British Austin's styling was too conservative for American tastes, the car was restyled by Count Alexis de-Sakhnoffsky, known for his more lavish bodies on Duesenbergs and Packards. Differences between the American and British versions included horizontal bonnet louvers, fixed disc wheels with detachable rims, larger headlamps, and more substantial fenders and bumpers. The roadster turned out to be especially cute. The American Austin's quite modern steel body used a minimum of wood.

Movie star Buster Keaton (right) taking delivery of an American Austin coupe. *National Automobile Museum Archives, Reno, Nevada*

'30-35 2-door coupe	★★★
'30-35 2-door roadster	★★★★★
'30-35 2-door pickup	★★★★
'30-35 2-door roadster pickup	★★★★
'30-35 2-door panel truck	★★★
'31-35 2-door business coupe	★★★★★
'31 2-door cabriolet	★★★★★
'33-35 2-door Suburban	★★★★

Body styles included a coupe and a roadster, plus several commercial models such as a sedan delivery, panel truck, and a completely open-top pickup that looked a bit like a jeep. A Suburban added in 1931 was really a coupe with a back seat for a couple of kids or a large dog. The rest of the American Austins were two-passenger vehicles.

The car got a lot of great press when early cars were purchased by celebrities such as Buster Keaton and Ernest Hemingway. Al Jolson bought the first coupe. The car was also the butt of vaudeville jokes and magazine cartoons. It appeared in movies, including *A Yankee in King Arthur's Court* and the ever popular Laurel and Hardy movie, *Our Wife*. They were used for advertising and delivery because of their attention-getting appeal and their economical operation.

The American Austin did everything well but sell. Whereas initial estimates projected annual sales of 60,000 to 100,000 units,

American Austin and American Bantam offered a large number of models. *Lillian J. Mitchell*

the actual numbers were far smaller. Only 8,558 cars had been produced by the end of 1930, and only 1,279 were made in 1931. The factory closed in the spring of 1932 with some 1,500 unfinished cars.

The American Austin probably would

The American Austin had a more substantial look compared to its British cousin, the Austin Seven. *Jim Conner*

have gone on to oblivion had it not been for Roy S. Evans, a successful automobile dealer in the South. Evans bought the existing inventory of 1,500 cars and quickly sold them in Florida for bargain-basement prices starting at $295. Then Evans took a big gamble by reopening the Butler plant. By the end of 1932, 3,846 American Austins had been built, mainly from components bought from suppliers who were happy to clean out their stock of Austin parts. Another 4,726 cars were built in 1933, but by the end of 1934, the production line stopped as the supply of parts was depleted and the company was in bankruptcy.

1939-42 American Bantam

By 1938, the company had been reorganized by Evans as the American Bantam Car Company, and the cars received a major restyling. Alexis deSakhnoffsky was called in again to update the styling, and he charged a mere $300. Tooling cost another $7,000. The new car featured an up-to-date

This 1940 American Bantam Sedan Delivery was purchased new by Syd LeSueur of Lakewood, Colorado, and he still owns it. For the first decade of its life, it earned a living in LeSueur's car repair business "chasing" parts, and it was towed behind customers' cars when they were picked up for and returned after service. *Bill Siuru*

American Austins and Bantams were bought by clowns and movie stars, but few "real" people. This 1940 American Bantam roadster is displayed at the Imperial Palace Auto Museum in Las Vegas, Nevada. *Bill Siuru*

'39-41 2-door coupe	★★★
'39-41 2-door roadster	★★★★★
'39-41 2-door pickup	★★★★
'39-41 2-door Boulevard Delivery	★★★★★
'39-41 2-door Speedster	★★★★★
'39-41 2-door panel truck	★★★★
'39-41 2-door station wagon	★★★★★
'40-41 2-door Hollywood	★★★★★
'40-41 2-door Riviera	★★★★★

styling with items like a horizontal bar grille that, depending on year and model, was either painted the body color or chrome-plated. There were also pontoon fenders, a smooth rear apron, and a restyled dash.

The Austin Seven-based mechanics were also revised. The engine was beefed up with Babbit bearings replacing the more expensive roller bearings, and an improved oil pump provided full-pressure lubrication. The three-speed transmission was synchronized on its top two gears, and the clutch provided smoother operation. There was a semifloating Hotckkiss-type rear axle with spiral bevel gears. Ross cam-and-lever steering replaced the antiquated Austin Seven design. The frame was also beefed up.

For 1940, the "Hill Master" engine got three-main bearings versus the previous two, was stroked to give 50.1cid (819cc) and 22hp, and reliability was improved. The company quoted a 0 to 30mph time of 5.5 seconds, a tribute to the car's light weight. Coupes and roadsters weighed just over 1,200lb. Top speed was about 60mph. Mechanical brakes were used to the end. For the 1940 cars, the headlights were moved from between the fender and grille to the top of the fenders.

Again there was a proliferation of models—sedans, station wagons, panel trucks, and three open-top models. The limited edition Riviera four-passenger convertible coupe was designed by Alex Tremulis, who would go on to design the Tucker. Another rare model was the two-passenger Hollywood convertible. The upscale 1939-40 Boulevard Delivery combined the front end of the roadster with a panel truck rear end. This upscale hauler featured items such as rear fender skirts and tiny carriage lights.

All this did not help, and the sales figures were much less than anticipated. Less than 7,000 American Bantams were built, and reportedly the company lost $75 on every car. About a third of the cars were exported, and they were popular in Australia, Europe, and South America. By 1941, production ceased for good but not before Bantam fathered the Bantam Reconnaissance

American Bantam employees testing an early version of the Bantam Reconnaissance Car, BRC), which featured four-wheel steering. *M. L. Rodgers*

Car that would evolve into the jeep. Too small to supply the nearly 600,000 jeeps built during World War II, the job was given to Willys-Overland and Ford. Bantam did manufacture 2,675 jeeps, most of which were lend-leased to the Russians.

Crosley

Powel Crosley, Jr., who had made millions with Crosley radios and Shelvador refrigerators, entered the automobile business in 1939. Much of Crosley's success came because he offered products at prices below the competition. The $19.95 Crosley radio was born when Crosley refused to pay over $100 for a radio in the early 1920s. Crosley's

A 1940 Crosley four-passenger convertible sedan. The side window frames are not removable. *Michael Bainter*

goal was to build a car that could be sold for as low as $325, far cheaper than most anything else sold in the United States.

1939-42 Crosley

The Crosley offered the ultimate in economy: a car with a two-cylinder, 38.9cid (637cc), air-cooled, 12hp at 4000rpm Waukesha engine. The Crosleys had a floor-shifted, three-speed transmission, and cable-activated mechanical brakes. The tiny cars rode on an 80in wheelbase, weighed around 1,000lb, and had 4.25x12 tires. Options were limited to a heater, a five-tube Crosley radio, and a tonneau cover for the convertibles.

Initially, the 1939 Crosleys came either as two- or four-passenger convertibles. A woodie station wagon, Covered Wagon, and panel delivery were added for 1940. The panel delivery was like the station wagon with a steel body and wood side panels, except the side windows were omitted. The commercial line was further expanded in 1941 with the addition of the Parkway Delivery and a pickup delivery. A chassis model was available on special order. The stroke of the engine was reduced for 1941 by 0.25in, giving a displacement of 35.3cid (574cc). The shorter stroke solved a weak crankshaft problem. Also, larger main bearings, improved oil cooling, and a U-joint in the driveline were used.

Crosley prices started at just $365, and they were first sold in appliance and hardware stores. After all, the 10ft long car did not take up that much space. By 1941, conventional dealerships were added. Crosley sold 7,000 cars before World War II. The Crosleys, with their 50mpg, 50mph top speed, and minimal tire wear became quite popular during the World War II years. They often sold for two, three, and sometimes even four times their original list prices.

'39-42 2-door convertible sedan/ coupe	★★★★
'40-41 2-door Covered Wagon	★★★★
'40-42 2-door station wagon	★★★★
'40-42 2-door panel delivery	★★★
'41-42 2-door pickup delivery	★★★
'41-42 2-door Parkway delivery	★★★

1946-52 Crosley

When car production resumed after World War II, all the American auto makers, except Kaiser-Frazer and Crosley, returned with warmed-over versions of prewar models. Kaiser/Frazer had new models because the company did not exist before the war. Crosley was the only established American auto maker to bring out an entirely new model. The 1946 Crosleys were new from the ground up.

The prototypes for the postwar Crosleys used an aluminum body and weighed only 1000lb. Crosley did not plan to paint the aluminum body, just give it an etched satin finish like an aircraft fuselage. Production vehicles using steel bodies weighed a few hundred pounds more.

During World War II, Crosley had obtained rights to a four-cylinder engine invented by Lloyd M. Taylor for urgent wartime needs, including use in portable generators and truck refrigerators. The engine's single overhead camshaft was driven via bevel gearing attached to a vertical shaft that ran between the crankshaft and camshaft. The 44cid (721cc), water-cooled, four-cylinder engine was rated at 26.5hp at 5400rpm, a real screamer compared to slow-turning contemporary American engines. The compression ratio ranged from 7.5:1 on 1946-48 models to 8:1 on 1951-52 cars. These Crosleys used a nonsynchromesh three-speed transmission with a floor-mounted gearshift.

Instead of being made of heavy forged castings, the cylinder block was formed from thin sheet metal stampings that were crimped together and then brazed into a monoblock by melting copper into all the joints and baking them in a hydrogen furnace. Crosley called the engine the COBRA for COpper BRAzed. The engine weighed a mere 58lb in basic form. When all the accessories were installed, the total weight was still well below 150lb. Aluminum was used on such items as pistons, intake manifold, and bell housing to help keep the weight down.

Unfortunately, the construction technique was not really designed for automo-

The unique Crosley ohc engine. That's Powel Crosley, Jr., holding the lightweight engine in short-block form. *Crosley*

tive use, where long life was needed. Because dissimilar metals were used, electrolysis ate holes in the cylinders, and they warped. Crosley reverted to a conventional cast iron block but kept the COBRA's design and dimensions. The replacement was called the CIBA engine, the letters signifying "cast iron block assembly" for obvious marketing reasons. The CIBA engine, weighing 221lb more, became optional on 1949 Crosleys, standard after 1950, and was retrofitted to earlier models, often at Crosley's expense.

'46-52 2-door sedan	★★★
'46-52 2-door convertible sedan	★★★★
'47-52 2-door station wagon	★★★
'47-52 2-door pickup	★★★
'47-51 2-door chassis and cab	★★★
'48-52 2-door panel delivery	★★★
'50-52 Farm-O-Road	★★★★

Many midget racers were powered by Crosley engines. *Bill Siuru*

The Crosley engines were among the most "hot-roddable" engines of their day. One of the most noted Crosley "tuners" was California's Nick Brajevich. This Crosley speed equipment manufacturer sold everything from special valve springs for the Crosley engines to full-race alcohol-burning engines. Using twin motorcycle carburetors, headers, Vertex magnetos, a hot cam, and by restroking and reboring, Nick was able to get 55hp at 8000rpm out of the engine. He

A 1950 Crosley Super two-door sedan with a custom, "aftermarket," two-tone paint scheme. *Bill Siuru*

built full race versions of the engine with a displacement of 53cid that made 60 horses on alcohol. However, the ultimate was a blown Crosley that turned out 75hp at a screaming 10,000rpm, using a Rootes-type supercharger. A Brajevich-built Crosley dragster was clocked at the century mark in the quarter-mile. In 1951, a Crosley-powered speedster hit 98mph at Bonneville.

Both Bandini and SIATA in Italy used the Crosley powerplant. The Crosley engine was equally at home in the water, dominating the under 48cid class in hydroplane racing for many years. The engine was also popular and successful in midget car racing for many years.

Along with Chrysler, Crosley introduced disc brakes in 1950. Its hydraulically powered brakes, appropriately called Hydradiscs, were like ones used on aircraft. Crosley did not spend enough time in developing the new brakes, and they had a tendency to jam when exposed to mud, road grime, and salt. By 1951, Crosley was using conventional drum brakes.

Crosley offered a full line of vehicles built around the same platform. Between 1946 and 1952, Crosley produced about 85,000 sedans, convertibles, station wagons, trucks, sports cars, and even a dual-purpose vehicle called the Farm-O-Road for the small farmer. Crosley even offered farm implements as options for the latter. The two-wheel-drive Farm-O-Road was fitted with a compound transmission that provided six speeds forward and two in reverse. The Farm-O-Road had a shorter 63in wheelbase, was 91.5in long, and had individual rear wheel braking so it could turn around, essentially in its own length. Even the regular Crosleys were agile, with an 80in wheelbase and overall length of 145 to 148in, about 15in less than a VW.

The postwar truck line consisted of pickups, a panel truck, and cab and chassis models that could be customized to meet the needs of the customer. These models included tiny fire engines for industrial use. Even though the trucks weighed about a third of the contemporary full-sized light trucks, they were rated with a 1/4-ton capacity.

The Crosley panel truck was essentially a station wagon without rear side windows. This is a 1949 model. *Crosley*

Where they came up short was in cargo volume. Crosley was the first to admit that they were designed for urban work.

The Crosley's economy could not be beat. Initial prices were as low as $800 and fuel economy was as high as 50mpg. Indeed, economy was the key word in Crosley advertising. The ads also made a point of "prompt delivery," a key consideration in the early postwar years.

The Crosley was restyled for 1949 with a new front end, which included a flatter hood, revised grille, wraparound bumper, squarer front fenders, reshaped wheel openings, and headlamps that were spaced more widely apart. For 1951, the Crosley was given a face-lift that consisted of a grille with a spinner in the center and V-shaped bumpers. After losing reportedly millions of his own money on this automotive venture, Powel Crosley ceased producing cars in July 1952.

1949-52 Crosley Hot Shot and 1951-52 Super Sports

In the early 1950s, Crosley was the only "major" American auto maker to offer a real sports car, and a good one at that. The Crosley Hot Shot first appeared in 1949, followed by the Super Hot Shot in 1950. The latter model was renamed the Super Sports in 1951. The chief difference between the Hot Shot and the Super Hot Shot/Super

Sports was a higher compression engine and better trim on the latter car. The Super Hot Shot/ Super Sports cars also came with doors that could be ordered as extra cost options on the base Hot Shot.

The compression ratio for the CIBA version of the Crosley four-cylinder, ohc engine was upped to an amazing 10:1 for this "performance" model. According to catalogs, it was an option on other Crosley models. Only the more reliable CIBA engine was used in the Crosley sports cars. The transmission was the standard, nonsynchromesh three-speed. At 137in, the Crosley sports cars were about 8in shorter than the standard Crosley cars and rode on an 85in wheelbase. This put the tiny 4.50x12 tires at the corners. Weighing in at 1,200 to 1,300lb, it was 700lb lighter than the higher powered contemporary MG-TD. The Crosley sports cars were priced in the range of $900 to $1,050, about half the price of the MG.

The rather antiquated semi-elliptical

Despite its rudimentary looks, the Crosley Hot Shot was a good performing, serious sports car. *Crosley*

front suspension and quarter-elliptics in the rear gave surprisingly good road handling and excellent cornering. Right out of the box, the performance Crosleys could turn in an honest 85mph. When *Mechanics Illustrated's* Tom McCahill tested a specially tuned Super Sports, he turned in 0 to 60mph times of under twenty seconds. He called it a "tin tub on wheels with a fine engine."

These were true "wind-in-your-face" sports cars in the classical British mold, including minimal weather protection offered by side curtains. The slab-sided car had bug-like headlamps, bucket seats of sorts, an outside mounted spare tire, and a flat windshield.

The Crosley sports cars were often class winners in the 500 to 750cc class and were successful in the SCCA H class through the early 1960s. A Super Sports won the Index of Performance in the inaugural running of the "12 hours of Sebring" in 1950, and Fritz Frierabend drove one to win the 750cc class of the Grand de la Suisse at an average speed of 51.5mph. Another special-bodied Crosley-powered car was averaging 73mph and well on its way to winning the Index of Performance in the 1951 LeMans 24-hour race when an electrical problem put it out. In this case, the engine had been modified for 42hp. Almost 2,500 Hot Shots, Super Hot Shots, and Super Sports had been built over a four-year period.

King Midget

Many will remember those tiny ads in the back of *Popular Science* for the "World's Number One Small Car." The ads referred to the King Midget, America's most successful postwar minicar, at least from the point of company survivability. The King Midgets were produced for almost a quarter-century, outlasting all the post-World War II upstarts. In some years, Midget Motors was the fifth largest American auto maker. Some 5,000 King Midgets were sold between 1946 and 1970. There were no King Midget dealers. Business was done primarily by U.S. mail. At peak production, a King Midget was produced each day.

'47-51 1-passenger roadster	★★★★
'51-57 2-passenger roadster	★★★
'57-70 2-passenger roadster	★★★
'70 Commuter	★★★★★

1947-50 King Midget

The King Midget was built by Claude Dry and Dale Orcutt in Athens, Ohio. Their first car was a single seater styled like a contemporary midget race car. It was powered by a single-cylinder, rear-mounted Wisconsin air-cooled 5 or 6hp engine. The first series of cars used an automatically operated centrifugal clutch as an option with a hand-operated clutch as standard equipment. There was no reverse. The 330lb car cost less than $500, or in kit form, only $270.

1951-70 King Midget

The completely redesigned King Midget, debuting in late 1951, was a much more practical car. Looking more like a real car, it could carry two people. It remained tiny, about a foot shorter than the wheelbase of contemporary Fords and Chevys. Power still came from a single-cylinder Wisconsin engine, now producing 7.5hp and 8.5hp on later models. Weight jumped to 450lb, the price was $550, and a kit was still available. Other features included mechanical brakes on the rear wheels, 4.00x8 (5.50x8 optional) tires, and a claimed 50 to 60mpg. Dry and Orcutt designed their own two-speed automatic transmission with reverse.

The restyled 1957 King Midget grew in overall length from 102 to 117in, and weight went up to 690lb and later 800lb. There were even finned rear fenders, and the car was fitted with doors but only side curtains. The Wisconsin single-cylinder, 23cid (377cc) engine now produced 9.25hp. Four-wheel hydraulic brakes were now used, and in 1961, the electrics were switched from 6 to 12-volt. The price breached the $1,000 mark. This model remained in production until 1970. In 1966 a Kohler single-cylinder, 29.1cid (476cc) engine was used; it was rated at 12hp.

Midget Motors produced a couple of "niche" market vehicles. In 1961, there was a Driving Training Car without a body. There was a model with hand controls for the

Eshelman—
America's Smallest "Mass-Produced" Car

Cheston L. Eshelman of Baltimore, Maryland, produced garden tractors, riding lawn mowers, rotary tillers, and a rudimentary motorscooter. Between 1953 and 1960, Eshelman also built cars for children and adults.

The Eshelman Child's Sports Car could carry a couple of children at speeds of up to 15mph. Looking like the pedal cars of the 1950s, it used a Briggs and Stratton, 2hp, single-cylinder engine mounted up front. The engine drove a pulley behind the seat using a V belt; the pulley was attached to a shaft running to a sprocket-and-chain setup that drove one or both of the rear wheels. There was an automatic recoil starter located on the dash, and it had an automatic clutch. A brake pedal operated the scrub shoes on the outside of the rear 10x2.75 tires. Eshelman claimed 70mpg and came fully assembled for around $295. While dimensions varied through the years, typically, the Child's Sports Car was 54in long, 24in wide, and 23in high.

The Adult's Sports Car was only a bit larger, being 64in long, 36in wide, and 32in tall. Styling mirrored that of the child's version, as did mechanics. The adult version did have four-wheel brakes, a parking brake, and larger tires (4.50x6). Also, there was a throttle pedal versus the hand throttle for the kids. Buyers had a choice of three Briggs and Stratton engines—2, 3, or 6hp. The latter provided a top speed of 30mph for a car that weighed 385lb without passengers. When fitted with full-sized, sealed-beam headlights and taillights for street use, the looks were weird to say the least.

The Eshelman Sportabout was a bit larger with a 72in overall length; it weighed 675lb, sold for $800, and was powered by a 8.4hp Briggs and Stratton engine. Sport abouts were marketed as golf carts to compete with electric ones. According to the ads, this was the only golf cart that could get up to "thirty-six holes to a gallon of gasoline."

Near the end, a "big" Eshelman 903 was developed with a two-cylinder engine. The two-passenger coupe included two doors with windows, an integral roof, a 30cu-ft capacity trunk, and tailfins. At $1,495, it was marketed as the lowest priced car built in the United States that could pass state inspection. Only a dozen Eshelman 903s were built. Much more successful were the Eshelman postal scooters supplied to the U.S. Post Office around 1959. About 3,500 of the three-wheel scooters were built for mail delivery.

An Eshelman Adult's Sports Car owned by Bill Hossfield of Ringwood, New Jersey. (*Bill Hossfield*)

Ads for Eshelman cars appeared in magazines like *Popular Science* and *Popular Mechanics* in the 1950s.

Ernest Freestone's award-winning 1964 King Midget. *Ernest Freestone*

One of a handful of 1970 King Midget Commuters built with definite dune-buggy looks. *John Weitlauf*

handicapped and a golf cart version.

While pretty spartan, there was a decent list of options. In early years, these included a tinted windshield, wood or aluminum winter doors with sliding plexiglass windows, hot air heater, speedometer, turn signals, extra-wide traction rear tires, special low gearing, foot rests on front fenders, and an extra-quiet muffler. Usually, there was only one standard color each year; other colors cost $10 more. By the mid-1960s, electric windshield wipers and washer, radio, carpeted panels, floor mats, and safety belts were added to the list. Philippine mahogany doors were offered in some years.

In 1966, Dry and Orcutt sold out to a new company headed by Joseph C. Stehlin which produced more cars than it could sell. A dwindling demand for minimal transportation spelled the end of this "survivor." The company was later sold to Vernon Eads, who tried to produce a completely redesigned 1970 Commuter with a fiberglass, dune buggy-like body. Only about five were produced before Ead went out of business, the result of under-capitalization and a ruinous fire.

Chapter 2

France

France's early postwar auto history was shaped by the "Plan Pons" that guided the recovery of the French auto industry after World War II. The plan limited the number of models French auto makers—Citroen, Peugeot, Renault, Simca, and Rovin—could produce. Only models needed to rebuild France's transportation system were included. With bureaucrats planning the products, economy and utility had high priority, and style and performance got low billing. Low-cost, high-mileage small cars were on the short list. The grand marques like Bugatti, Delahaye, and Delage were not even on the list but were left to flounder and eventually fail. Hotchkiss, Ford, and Panhard were also not in the "grand

Early Citroen 2CVs had corrugated hoods, carry-overs from the prototypes whose entire front end looked like a metal shed. *Citroen*

French Microcars of the
Early Post-World War II Period

The French produced some of the most unique microcars to meet the challenges of poor economic conditions, limited gasoline, and devastation after World War II. A few reached production, albeit in small numbers.

The two-seat 1951 Atlas roadster looked like a large child's 1940s-style pedal car. Originally called the *La Coccinelle*, the 600lb car had a single-cylinder 175cc engine, doorless fiberglass body, and a top speed of 40mph.

The 1946-49 Julien was a nicely styled, two-seat convertible powered by a rear-mounted 325cc single-cylinder engine driving the rear wheels via a single chain. The 113in long car had a narrower tread in the rear than in the front. Top speed for the 660lb car was around 45mph.

The 1951-54 Reyonnah folded for parking. The front wheels were mounted on folding sponsons to reduce the tread of the front wheels to correspond to the narrow fixed tread of the rear ones. On the road, the Reyonnah was 60in wide; parked, only 30in wide. The 114in-long car looked a bit like a Messerschmitt, including the side-hinged canopy opening for access to the tandem seats. Power came from a 175cc Ydral or a 250cc AMC engine mounted in the rear and driving the rear wheels.

Charles Mochet built the Velocar human-powered vehicle from 1918 through 1951. They were especially popular in fuel-starved, German-occupied France. In 1951, a rear-mounted 100cc engine was used in the Velocar. It still rode on bicycle-style wheels, and only the rear

wheels had brakes. This grew into the Type CM Luxe with a 125cc Yral engine. A rudimentary body covered a simple tubular frame, and the front wheels were independently sprung. The 95in car could hit 30mph. At its peak, Mochet was selling as many as forty cars a month. In 1956, Mochet offered a more conventional looking, four-passenger, slab-sided two-door sedan. There was a 175cc engine still in the rear, and it had a top speed of 37mph. Like the Velocars, the rear wheels were more closely spaced than the front wheels.

The tiny two-passenger 1938-52 Rolux was introduced prior to World War II but did not become popular until the postwar mini-car boom. About 1,000 were sold. This very basic car came without doors or top. Power for the 104in-long car came from a rear-mounted 125cc, single-cylinder, air-cooled engine. Top speed was only about 35mph.

Rosengart began by building Austin Sevens under license in 1928 and returned to the small car market in 1952 with the Ariette and Artisane saloons and drophead coupes. These cars combined the Austin Seven 747cc engine with modern slab-sided styling and an updated chassis. At nearly twice the price of a Citroen 2CV, only a few hundred were sold. The 1954 Sagaie was a slightly restyled Ariette done in fiberglass and had a CEME motorcycle engine. About two hundred Ariette bodies were also sold to Panhard, which installed its 850cc, flat-twin engine and sold it as the Panhard Starlet.

The tiny, 110in-long, doorless 1946 Rovin looked like a child's toy. However, Rovin became the most popular postwar French

The 1947 Rovin D2 came without doors and had a 260cc engine in the rear. *Kai Bremer*

The Mochet definitely showed its pedal car heritage. *Jesse Patton*

minicar. The two-seat roadster had a single headlight in the center of the hood. By 1947, the Rovin D2 reached limited production now with conventional headlights and slightly modified styling. Power came from a single-cylinder, 260cc, air-cooled engine in the rear that drove the rear wheels via a chain and shaft drive system. Top speed was 45mph. In 1948, the Rovin grew to the 120in-long Rovin Type D3. The engine was now water-cooled, had two-opposed cylinders, and rated at 10hp. There was a three-speed transmission, rack and pinion steering, and cable-operated mechanical brakes on all wheels. The fully independent suspension system used two transverse leaf springs in the front and coil-spring swing axles in the rear. The new slab-sided unit body featured doors with wind-up windows. The final Rovin was the Model D4, which appeared in 1952 and used an opposed twin-cylinder, 462cc, water-cooled engine that produced 13hp. A top speed of just over 50mph was claimed, and it had grown another 4in in overall length. Production of Rovins ended in 1958.

Gabriel Voisin was already famous in aviation before he began building great cars in 1918. His tiny Biscooter (Biscouter) had front-wheel drive and a traverse-mounted engine up front. Top speed was 40mph. By 1951, the Biscooter was being produced in Spain. The Biscooters used a 197cc, single-cylinder Hispano-built Villiers engine. It came as a roadster, coupe, van, and woodie station wagon. In 1956, a fiberglass sports coupe was offered, though few were built.

It is hard to believe anyone would take the Biscooter as a serious car, but some 5,000 Spaniards did between 1951 and 1958. At one point, it was the most popular Spanish-built car.

plan." Of these, only Panhard produced a minicar, and a very innovative one at that.

Citroen

Andre Citroen began building cars in 1919. In 1934, Citroen brought out its famous *traction avant*, and from that point forward, Citroen would "march to the beat of a different drummer." Citroen covered both ends of the market with unique products. *traction avant*, DS21, and Citroen-Maserati SM offered advanced technology and luxury. The 2CV and its derivatives provided basic transportation.

1949-90 Citroen 2CV

Of the successful "people's" cars, the Citroen 2CV was the most unique. Developed just before World War II, the 2CV represented basic transportation in its simplest form. Citroen engineers, lead by Pierre-Jules Boulanger, were tasked with designing a car to sell for about one-third the price of the other French cars. It had to carry "four people under an umbrella" plus 110lb of luggage at 35mph, be very economical and reliable, and ride so smooth that it could "carry a basket of eggs across a freshly plowed field without a single egg being broken." The 2CV did all this and more.

While 250 prototypes were built, all but a handful were crushed, so they would not fall into the hands of the occupying Germans. The *deux chevaux* was shown to the public in 1948. Initially, it was ridiculed, and the "experts" called it ugly. The public saw differently; even as late as 1954, there was a two-and-a-half-year wait.

'49-70 2CV 4-door sedan (375cc/425cc)	★★★★
'70-90 2CV6 4-door sedan (602cc)	★★★★
'58-67 Sahara 4x4	★★★★★
'51-78 Truckette/station wagon	★★★★
'59-64 Bijou 2-door coupe	★★★★★
'61-78 Ami 6/8 4-door sedan/ station wagon	★★
'68-83 Dyane 4/6 4-door sedan	★★
'68-88 Mehari	★★★
'79-88 Mehari 4x4	★★★★

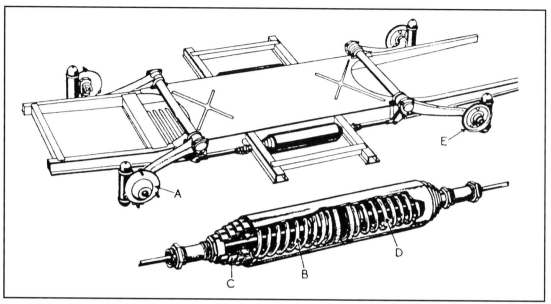

The 2CV's unique suspension system. When the front wheel (A) strikes a bump, its connecting rod compresses the coil spring (B). This draws the cylindrical casing forward against the action of spring (C) and partially compresses the rear wheel spring (D), bracing the rear wheel (E) to resist the shock of the bump. Like the rest of the car, the system was simple but worked well. *Citroen*

Whenever Citroen planned to cease production, there was an outcry, and production would continue for a few more years. After production ceased in France in 1988, production was set up in Portugal where manufacturing lasted into mid-1990. Some seven million 2CVs and derivatives were produced. It was also produced in nineteen countries, from Argentina and Iran to South Vietnam and Uruguay.

The 2CV body had a minimum of curves and complex features. Doors, fenders, rear deck lid, seats, and other parts easily unbolted for repair or to turn the 2CV into a small truck. The huge fabric sunroof rolled back like a sardine can top. Up until early 1970,

Later 2CVs, like this 1968 model, gained a third side window, two-tone paint jobs, and plusher interiors. *Bill Siuru*

The 2CV station wagon was just a Truckette with windows and rear seats. *A. Meyer*

24

the rear trunk also had a roll-up fabric cover, though metal trunk lids appeared earlier with the A2LP in 1957. Until 1960, simple but quite comfortable fabric-over-rubber-band seats were used.

The twin-cylinder, four-stroke, air-cooled engine drove the front wheels. Originally, displacement was only 375cc to produce 9hp at 3500rpm. In 1954, the engine was increased to 425cc, and horsepower was 12 at 3500rpm. By 1970, there was another displacement, and power increased to 602cc and, depending on the year, 21 to 29hp. In reference to the 602cc engine, the last models were called the 2CV6. Early 375cc cars had a top speed of only 40mph, but the last cars were capable of speeds above 70mph but took awhile to get there.

The basic weight of the 2CV was about 1,100lb. The 2CV had a fully synchronized four-speed transmission with fourth gear being an overdrive. The car's smooth ride came partly from the relatively long 94.4in wheelbase. With the wheels at the corners, the 2CV had an overall length of only 149in. Also helping was the unique, fully independent suspension.

To compensate for different loadings, the headlight's aim could be adjusted from inside the car. While initial prototypes had a single headlight, production models had two, so 2CVs would not be mistaken for motorcycles. The interior was beyond spartan.

Early versions had only an ammeter and a speedometer, the latter coupled with the windshield wiper drive, which was driven off the transmission. The brakes were four-wheel hydraulic drum, the front ones being inboard. After 1981, 2CVs had front disc brakes.

Through the years, Citroen made changes to the styling. For example, a third side window was added for better rearward visibility. Upscale versions, such as the Charleston, appearing in 1981, and the Dolly, in 1986, featured more creature comforts and two-tone paint schemes. There were also a pickup, produced in England, a station wagon, and a Truckette panel truck.

When Citroen wanted a 4x4, it put a second 425cc engine in the 2CV's trunk to create the Sahara. The front engine still drove the front wheels, while the rear one drove the rear wheels. There were two separate transmissions, clutches, ignition and starting systems, and fuel pumps. A single throttle pedal controlled both engines, and a single pedal worked both clutches. A central, floor-mounted lever controlled both transmissions simultaneously. Except for off-road driving, only the front engine was used. In case of failure, the rear one could be used alone. Some 694 Saharas were built.

Citroens were assembled in Slough, England. Besides putting the steering wheels on the right side and making

The 2CV Sahara was distinguished by the spare on the hood and fuel filler spouts in the doors for the dual fuel tanks under the seats. *Deux Chevaux Club of Great Britain*

The British-built Citroen Bijou was pure 2CV underneath. Costing about 20 percent more than the ordinary 2CV, it was not a hot seller. *Deux Chevaux Club of Great Britain*

modifications for the British market, the Slough plant produced a 2CV model made nowhere else. This was the 1959-64 Bijou two-door hardtop. Underneath the rather handsome fiberglass body were 2CV mechanics, including the 425 cc engine. Inside, there were the rubber webbing seats, though the folddown rear seat was only for "occasional" use. There was a more modern instrument panel and a new single-spoke DS-style steering wheel.

1961-78 Ami 6/8

On several occasions, Citroen tried to replace the 2CV with updated cars like the Ami and Dyane, based on 2CV mechanics. The 2CV outlasted them all! The Ami borrowed the 2CV's unique interacting suspension system, inboard front brakes, and 94.25in wheelbase, though the Ami was a few inches longer. The Ami 6 used the 602cc engine, and the Ami 8 appeared in 1969 with a 32hp engine. A four-door sedan and station wagon were offered. Styling quirks included adjustable rectangular Cibie headlights, a "scoop-down" hood, and a backwards slanting rear window on sedans. The steel-unitized body had a reinforced fiberglass roof.

1968-83 Dyane 4 and 6

Citroen updated the 2CV's unique look with the Dyane, which had smoother lines, square headlights mounted in the fenders, and a rear hatch. Like the 2CV, there was a

A station wagon version of the Ami was available after 1966. *A. Meyer*

While the 2CV had "character," the 2CV-based Dyane did not and was not that popular with the French. *Citroen*

large fabric sunroof and flat windshield. The Dyane 4 used the 425cc, 18hp, two-cylinder engine while the Dyane 6 had the 602cc engine rated at 25hp. The Dyane 4 was dropped after 1974, but the Dyane 6 continued until 1983. An Acadienne panel truck was also built off the Dyane.

1968-88 Mehari

The Mehari was Citroen's version of the Volkswagen Thing and BMC Mini-Moke. The Mehari had a body made of eleven plastic panels that were fastened to a tubular frame that, in turn, was bolted to the platform chassis. The Mehari used a 602cc engine that produced 25hp. In 1979, a four-wheel-drive version of the Mehari was added. The 4x4 Mehari had a four-speed gearbox with three reduced gear ratios as well.

In 1975, Citroen was bought out by Peugeot. In the 1970s, the Citroen LN and LNA used the two-cylinder, air-cooled engines in Peugeot bodies. This was followed in 1978 by the Visa, which used the air-cooled flat-twin, the Peugeot floor pan, and a new body. Later, a four-cylinder Peugeot engine was offered as an option.

Citroens were built in Romania under the Oltcit label and in Yugoslavia as the Tomos. Romanian-built cars included a version of the Visa with either a 652cc two-cylinder or 1129cc flat-four. Romanian-built

Rather than somewhat fragile fiberglass, the Citroen Mehari used a more rugged thermoplastic material called ABS Cycolac. *Citroen*

The Citroen LN used the two-cylinder, air-cooled Citroen engine in an updated Peugeot body. *Citroen*

cars were sold as the Axel in Western Europe.

Panhard

Panhard et Levassor was one of the world's oldest auto makers, producing its first cars in 1891. Before World War II, Panhard built only larger cars. While postwar Panhards were not tiny, they were all powered by two-cylinder, air-cooled engines.

During the occupation, Panhard worked on a small car with either a 250cc or 350cc horizontally opposed, twin-cylinder engine driving the front wheels. The concept was very similar to a design done by premier front-wheel-drive advocate Jean-Albert Gregoire. Along with Pierre Fenaille, Gregoire built the 1926-32 Tracta, the first front-wheel-drive car to be built in significant numbers. Gregoire patents were used on pioneering front-wheel-drive cars such as the Adler, Citroen, and DKW.

The Gregoire design was the Aluminum Francois-Gregoire (AF-G), developed in secrecy during the war. The Aluminum part came because it was developed in cooperation with l'Aluminium Francais and used aluminum extensively. Panhard's designers used the best features of the Panhard design

'48-53 Dyna X (100/110/120/130) 4-door sedan	★★★
'51-53 Dyna X (100/110/120/130) cabriolet	★★★★★
'52-56 Junior roadster/cabriolet	★★★★★
'53-59 Dyna Z 4-door sedan	★★★
'56-59 Dyna Z 2-door cabriolet	★★★★★
'59-65 PL 17 4-door sedan	★★★
'59-65 PL 17 2-door cabriolet	★★★★★
'63-67 24 (A, B, BT, C, CT,) 2-door sedan	★★★★
add one-half star for Tigre option	

and AF-G prototype to create the VP2, which evolved into the Dyna, debuting in 1946. This prototype established the basic design for the rest of the days of the marque. Panhard did not even acknowledge Gregoire's contribution, but licenses to the AF-G design were sold to Kaiser-Frazer, Hartnett in Australia and Kendall in England; none went into production.

1947-53 Dyna Panhard 100, 110, 120, and 130

While some fifty preproduction Dyna Panhards were built in 1947, regular production did not begin until 1948. The initial Dyna X was a four-door sedan with suicide front doors and sliding glass side windows. The unique front end design was dictated by the engine layout. The two-cylinder, 610cc, 25hp, air-cooled, four-stroke, flat-twin engine was combined with the four-speed synchromesh transmission to supply power to the front wheels. The whole unit was mounted forward of the front wheels. The Dyna X used aluminum extensively, including not only an all-aluminum body but a shell and cowl as well. The chassis was steel. Trim and bumpers were polished aluminum. The first series was designated the Dyna 100 type X84, the "100" for the top speed in kilometers-per-hour.

Two new models were added in 1950, a two-door cabriolet and a berline *decouvrable*, a four-door sedan with a fabric sunroof. Also in 1950, the engine was substantially redesigned, and horsepower was upped to 28. Top speed was 110km/h, and it was now

The Panhard X series, built between 1947 and 1953, was Panhard's first small car. *Les Amis de Panhard*

called the Dyna 110 type X85. By April 1950, there was a larger 745cc, 34hp engine, so the Dyna 120 could compete with the popular, and similar looking, Renault 4CV.

A 750 Sprint version of the engine offered 38hp. The final model to use the original body style was the Dyna 130 with an 851cc, 40 to 42hp engine that appeared in mid-1951. When production of the Dyna X-series ceased in 1953, some 45,000 cars had been built.

1952-56 Dyna Junior

Several specialty coachbuilders created more sporting models using the Panhard Dyna X-series flat-twin engine or the complete engine and chassis. One prototype by Di Rosa was put into production in 1952 as the Panhard Dyna Junior. It was available either as a two-seat roadster or cabriolet with roll-up windows.

While using the same 84in wheelbase as the Dyna X sedans, the Junior was only 145in long. It was initially powered by the 38hp, 750cc Sprint engine. With a steel body, it weighed 1,600lb and took over twenty-six seconds to accelerate to 60mph. Shortly, it was offered with an 851cc engine, though the 745cc engine was still available for 750cc class racing. The ultimate Dyna Junior used a MAG supercharger to boost output to 60hp, giving a near 90mph top speed.

The Dyna Junior was a moderately attractive and performing sports car built off the Panhard X series. *Les Amis de Panhard*

1953-65 Dyna Z and PL 17

The Panhard was totally restyled for 1954 with a "jelly bean" look. With a 101in wheelbase and an overall length of 180in, the new Dyna Z was far from a small car, at least by European standards. The long wheelbase plus the mounting of the engine and transmission ahead of the front wheels meant seating for six passengers.

The Dyna Z continued to use an aluminum/magnesium body, but unlike the Dyna X cars, there were no aluminum castings for the shell. Instead, there was a rigid floor pan with sturdy side rails joined to the front and rear substructures. Then advanced technology argon-arc welding was used to assemble the components of the semimonocoque body.

The engine, clutch, four-speed transmission, front-wheel-drive differential, rack and pinion steering, twin transverse leaf independent suspension, drum brakes, and wheels were attached with six bolts. Five bolts attached the rear unit consisting of wheels, drum brakes, and open V-section rigid rear axle suspended by triple transverse torsion bars. The resulting car weighed

The Dyna-Panhard Z-series was one of the first cars to have a rounded "jelly bean" look. This 1959 Dyna-Panhard Deluxe, with a Detroit-style two-tone paint scheme, is owned by Rich Bachmann. *Rich Bachmann*

This 1964 Panhard PL17 cabriolet shows the facelift that distracted somewhat from the Dyna-Panhard's original clean lines. *Les Amis de Panhard*

only about 1,500lb of which the whole chassis contributed an amazingly low 202lb.

While the body and chassis were new, the air-cooled flat-twin was still used. The 851cc engine was rated at 42hp at 5000rpm, and an 85mph top speed was claimed mainly because of the excellent aerodynamics. However, it took almost a half-minute to go from 0 to 60mph. Fuel mileage was an excellent 40 to 45mpg.

Helping performance was the optional Tigre engine in 1959. The Tigre produced 50hp at 5200rpm through changes like a two-barrel carburetor (it later went back to a single barrel with no loss of power), a high-performance camshaft, a new distributor, a stronger crankshaft, and lighter connecting rods.

Unfortunately, the cars started putting on weight as steel replaced aluminum to cut costs. For the 1956 models, except for the hood, doors, and trunk lid, steel was used for the body and chassis. The next year, everything was made of steel, and the Dyna 57 weighed over 200lb more than the Dyna 54. Numbers in the Dyna Z's designation corresponded to the model year.

Like many other European auto makers, Panhard offered clutchless driving with its "Jaeger coupler" electromagnetic clutch. The four-speed was column-shifted, and the Dyna Z had a rather quirky-looking control console straddling the steering column, with all the switches located around the steering wheel. Plastics were used extensively.

Besides the four-door sedan, there was also a neat-looking Dyna Z cabriolet. Other models included station wagons, trucks, and vans. Through the years of production 1953 to 1959, in different markets, there were a variety of trim packages going under names like Luxe, Luxe Special, Grande Luxe, Vendome, Seine Sedan, Grand Standing, and so forth. Some of the packages included two-tone paint schemes that were less than flattering to the Dyna Z's basic styling.

The PL 17 that replaced the Dyna Z series in 1959 was just a major facelift. Since body sculpturing was "in" at the time, the PL 17 featured it at both ends. Aluminum trim was also added above the headlights, and an aluminum strip ran across the hood between the headlamps hiding a welded seam. Strips were added to the front fenders, and there were horizontal fins over the taillamps. A rectangular slit replaced the former oval air intake for the engine.

The PL 17 Luxe was a base model, whereas the Grand Standing, complete with its two-tone paint job often in outrageous colors, was the upscale model. Later models used names like Nice and Monte Carlo. Two versions of the 851cc engine were offered; the base version was rated at 42hp at 5000rpm. In 1962 there was a slight displacement decrease, from 851cc to 848cc. The optional Tigre was rated at 60hp at 5300rpm. The Tigre option included an interior done in a tiger-skin motif, in 1959 and 1960. After 1961, normal front-hinged doors replaced previous suicide-hinged ones.

1963-67 24 series

The 24 series that went on sale in the fall of 1963 was Panhard's swan song. The Panhard 24, which came in only two-door form, had a definite Citroen look, as might be expected from the Citroen-Panhard marriage of a few years previous. In the mid-1950s, Citroen had obtained a 25 percent share of Panhard et Levassor. Indeed, by 1966 the 24 was sold alongside Citroens because Citroen had acquired the remainder of the Panhard shares in 1965. While looking like an airy hardtop coupe, the 24's thin B-pillars were fixed. Struts inside the A- and C-pillars supported the roof. Originally, there were the 24 C and 24 CT 2+2 coupes. The 24 C and CT used a 90in wheelbase, compared to 101.5in on the PL17 four-door sedans. In 1965, the wheelbase and body were stretched by about 10in. Since the added length occurred between the rear edge of the door and the rear wheel opening, the new 24 B and 24 BT models became full-fledged four-passenger sedans.

While the styling was all-new, the mechanics underneath were still Panhard Dyna. The 24 C and B used a 50hp version of the 848cc, flat twin. The more sporty 24 CT "Coupe Tigre" and 24 BT "Berline Tigre" models got 10 more horsepower from the Tigre version. The Tigre versions also got a more sporty instrument panel with a round speedometer and tachometer. While the 24 C was discontinued in 1965, the 24 BT, C, and CT were continued to the end. In 1966, there was a 24 A built on the long wheelbase but with a simplified interior and a minimal external trim.

Renault

During the years when European imports reigned supreme in the United States, Renault was usually in second place behind Volkswagen in number of cars sold. However, there was usually a huge difference in these numbers. Compared to the millions of VWs, Renault imported a total of about a quarter million cars in the 1950s and 1960s.

'47-61 4CV 4-door sedan	★★★
'47-57 4CV "Specials"	★★★★★
'57-68 Dauphine 4-door sedan	★★★
'57-62 Gordini/Dauphine	★★★★
'59-68 Floride/Caravelle	★★★★
'57-68 Dauphine "Specials"	★★★★★
'62-72 R8/R8 Major 4-door sedan	★★
'65-70 R8 Gordini 4-door sedan	★★★★★
'61-89 Renault 4/4L 4-door hatchback	★★
'72-80 Renault 5/Le Car 2-door hatchback	★
'81-83 Renault 5 4-door hatchback	★

The Panhard 24 was the marque's final model. This is a later 24 CT version. *Les Amis de Panhard*

1947-61 Renault 4CV

The Renault 4CV, along with the Citroen 2CV, were the right cars to provide transportation in France immediately after World War II. The 4CV, or *la Quatre Chevaux*, developed in secrecy during the war, was first shown in 1946. Contrary to 4CV folklore, Ferdinand Porsche was not involved in the 4CV's design. The 4CV prototype was shown to Professor Porsche who was being held prisoner by the French. Porsche, who was in poor health, did not do anything more than look at the 4CV, which was too close to production for any major changes. For instance, just before production commenced, it was discovered that the headlights were 50mm too low according to French law. The solution? The law was changed.

The first cars were painted desert sand yellow, using paint left over from Rommel's Afrika Korps. No other paint was available. In the following year, some black 4CVs were built. When production ceased in 1961, 1,105,499 4CVs had been built. In addition, more 4CVs were produced in England, Belgium, Ireland, Australia, South Africa, Spain, and under license by Hino in Japan.

The 4CV used a rear-mounted, 760cc, four-cylinder, 19hp, water-cooled, ohv engine. There was a three-speed transmission, with only the top two gears synchronized, drum brakes, rack and pinion steering, and unit-body construction. The fully independent suspension system used coil springs and swing axles in the rear. The 4CV had an

83in wheelbase, an overall length of 143in, and rode on 5.00x15 tires. Top speed was 60mph, and it could deliver 40 to 50mpg. While the prototypes had only two doors that were hinged at the front, the production 4CVs had four doors, the front ones being of the suicide variety. Up until 1961, side windows were of the sliding type; after that, windup windows were used in the front doors. Through the years of production, there were several levels of trim, Standard, Luxe, Grand Luxe, and Super Grand Luxe. The convertible, or *decapotable*, was a four-door sedan with a large fabric sunroof.

Deutch—Bonnet

Automobiles Deutch-Bonnet was not "officially" founded until 1947, though the relationship between Charles Deutch and Rene Bonnet dated back to 1932. DB's first Dyna-Panhard-based car was a Formula 3 racer of which fifteen copies were produced. DB began "series" production of its GT coupes in 1952. Until 1955, they had aluminum bodies done by Frua of Italy. Then they used fiberglass bodies on a tube frame chassis. The GT coupes rode on an 85in wheelbase and were only about 160in long. Both two-place and 2+2 coupes were listed, and a few roadsters were built. More interested in performance than names, DB rather randomly used titles like HBR4, HBR5, GT Luxe, Sports Saloon, Grand Turismo Sports Coupe, DB-Panhard, DB 750, GT 1000, and so forth. Power for all came from Panhard air-cooled, flat-twin engines. DB was able to obtain 30hp from the 610cc version. With displacement increases to 1100cc and 1300cc, output was upped to 60hp and 65hp, respectively. However, most DBs had 744cc or 851cc versions. In standard form, these two engines produced 46hp and 51hp (56hp after 1958), respectively. Modified versions were tuned to produce as much as 56hp (745cc), 58hp (850cc), and 80hp (954cc).

DB's four-speed had a shift pattern that took a bit to get used to because DB adapted the column shifter used in Panhards to a more sports-car-like floor shifter. The front independent suspension used upper and lower transverse leaf springs. In the rear, torsion bars were used. There was rack and pinion steering, and drum brakes were used, though disc brakes were available after 1955.

While the body was modified through the years of production, 1952 through 1961, the fastback coupe kept its excellent aerodynamic look and efficiency. Some early models had three Buick-like portholes on the front fenders;

later ones used more attractive rectangular air vents. Pop-up headlamps on early models gave way to plexiglass covered ones in 1956. The less than 50in tall coupes had wraparound windshields, large side windows, wide doors, and often came with two-tone paint jobs.

Panhard joined with DB to enhance its performance image through motorsports victories. For instance, DBs won class victories at Le-Mans three times ('54, '55, and '56) and the Index of Performance at the LeMans five times ('54, '56, '59, '60, and '61). There were class victories at Sebring ('52 and '53), four in the Mille Miglia between '52 and '57, and two in the Irish Tourist Trophy ('54 and '55). It was also a major contender in the America's SCCA's H-production class in its day.

As with Panhard, Citroen had gained a partial interest in DB by 1955. After three decades of partnership, Bonnet and Deutch parted ways following a disagreement in late 1961. For a short period, Bonnet built cars under his own name, mainly the Rene Bonnet-Djet, powered by a Renault four-cylinder engine.

The HBR5 and the HBR4 were Deutch-Bonnet's best sellers, with some 660 built and about one hundred sold in the United States. *(Jean-Yves Lardinois)*

Regular sedans could be ordered with a small, metal sliding sunroof.

In 1951, the displacement of the engine was slightly decreased to 747cc, but horsepower was increased to 23. By 1958, horsepower was upped to 28, and top speed approached 70mph. In 1955, the Ferlec automatic clutch became available on 4CV. With Ferlec, the clutch was electrically disengaged when you touched the gearshift. Gear selection still had to be done manually.

Many "specials" were built off the *la Quartre*. The Ghia-designed Resort Special 4CV offered in the early 1960s was Renault's beach buggy. Some of the more handsome specials included the Autobleau 4CV two-door hardtop done by Ghia and a neat Autobleau cabriolet from Henri Chapron. Maille also made a two-door hardtop off the 4CV, which retained more of the 4CV's body panels, and Labourdette modified the 4CV into

a "cute" two-place cabriolet. Motto of Turin turned the 4CV into a very Italian-looking fastback coupe. The ATLA used a fiberglass coupe body, complete with Mercedes-Benz 300SL-type gullwing doors on the 4CV platform.

1956-68 Renault Dauphine

The Dauphine, introduced in 1956, was also called the Renault 5CV and originally called the Corvette, a name dropped early for obvious reasons. While the mechanics underneath the Dauphine's prettier unibody were like the 4CVs, the Dauphine was a bit larger, with an 89in wheelbase and had a 155in overall length. The Dauphine's four-cylinder engine was based on the 4CV unit but with a 845cc displacement.

Initially, the engine produced 32hp and was mated to a three-speed transmission, again without first gear being synchronized. The Ferlec semi-automatic was available from the start, and after 1963, there was a fully automatic transmission. The automatic was unique in that a magnetic powder took the place of the fluid coupling used in other automatic transmissions. The transmission's outer drum was connected to the engine while an inner hub was connected to the three-speed transmission. The thin air gap between the two was filled with a fine iron powder. When an electric current energized the magnetic field, the powder essentially solidified, causing the entire setup to move as a single unit. Renault used push buttons

The Renault 4CV's mechanical design greatly influenced Renaults through the 1970s. *Renault*

The Dauphine was Renault's answer to the VW Beetle. While prettier, the four-door provided less performance than did the Beetle. *Bill Siuru*

on the dashboard for gear selection. Finally, the manual's first gear was synchronized by 1962, and a four-speed was optional by 1963. By 1964, four-wheel disc brakes became standard, a first in the economy field. Only a four-door sedan was available, but it could be ordered with a sliding metal sunroof.

Through the years Renault and after-

Alpine

The Alpines were successful sports cars based on Renault mechanics. Societe des Automobiles Alpine was founded in 1955 by Jean Redele who campaigned a modified 4CV to victories at Monte Carlo and in the Mille Miglia. His 1954 victories in Coupes des Alpes and a 750cc class win in the Mille Miglia were commemorated by naming the marque Alpine and its first model in 1955 the A106 Mille Miles.

The A106 was based on uprated 4CV mechanics, including its platform chassis, 747cc engine, and three-speed transmission. A five-speed was optional. By 1956, the A106 could be ordered with the Renault Dauphine 845cc engine or 904cc and 948cc variations. The A106's somewhat stubby fiberglass two-seat coupe body, a convertible came in 1957, was designed with help from Michelotti. A106s were built until 1960.

The A108 went into production in 1957, still using Renault mechanics, but was now built around Alpine's own tubular backbone chassis under the fiberglass body. Initially coming in cabriolet form in 1961, it was joined by a 2+2 coupe and Berlinette Tour de France versions. Engines included a 998cc developing 77hp in 1961, and by 1964, the 1108cc engine was tuned by Gordini to produce 87hp.

The A110 was Alpine's longest running model (1963-73) and again was based on Renault mechanics with a fiberglass body and tubular steel backbone chassis. Initially, the A110 was powered by the 998cc Renault engine as used concurrently in the A108 but was soon replaced by the Gordini-tuned 1108cc engine. Through the A110's lifetime, other four-cylinder engines were available, including 1108cc, 95hp; 1255cc, 103hp; 1296cc, 120 and 130hp; 1609cc, 140hp; and an ultimate factory rally car version with 1800cc pumping out over 170hp.

Other features included four-wheel disc brakes and rack and pinion steering. Many A110s used stock Renault four-speeds but could be ordered with a five-speed. The front suspension used upper and lower control arms, coil springs, and an antiroll bar. In the rear, there were swing axles, trailing radius arms, and coil springs.

Two body styles were offered, which were styled again by Michelotti. The GT4 was a 2+2 coupe with wraparound windshield and rear window, front vent windows, and rather large rear quarter windows. The Berlinette was a two-seat coupe that looked like the GT4, but there were significant differences above the beltline, including a steeper slanting windshield, a rear window with a deeper wraparound, and revised side windows that slanted rearward. The French-blue A110s were very successful in motorsports competition, for instance, taking the first three places in the 1971 Monte Carlo Rally, another first at Monte Carlo in 1973, and World Rally Championship in 1973, surprisingly in its last year of production.

In the 1960s, Alpine grew from about one hundred cars a year in 1963 to five hundred to six hundred cars annually by the end of decade. Alpines were also produced in Brazil, Bulgaria, Mexico, and Spain. In 1971, Alpine assumed responsibility for Renault's motorsports program, and by 1974, Alpine had been taken over by Renault.

The Alpine A110s made the most of the parts in the Renault parts bin. *Chris Alford Racing and Sports Cars*

market tuners offered special versions of the Dauphine. Some had cosmetic enhancements, others made the Dauphine go faster and handle better. The Renault Ondine offered in the United States in 1961 and 1962 was a luxury variant with a four-speed gearbox, special wheels, and an interior by Van Clecf-Arpels. Henri-Chapron produced about a hundred Dauphine *decapotables*.

In 1957, Renault had Amedee Gordini "tune" the 845cc engine. Cylinder head, carburetor, and manifold changes boosted the horsepower to 38. A few of the Gordinis were fitted with a close-ratio four-speed, and most went into the hands of racers.

In 1961 and 1962, Renault offered another Gordini version with power upped to 40hp. In comparison to the ordinary Dauphines, top speed went from 70mph to 80mph, and the 0 to 60mph time took 22.3 seconds, shaving a whole 12 seconds from the regular Dauphine's snail's pace. To distinguish a Gordini from a regular Dauphine, there was a special green-and-black steering wheel and "GORDINI" emblems on the front fenders. While the Gordini name was dropped after 1962, many of its features were still available as options, including deluxe trim, 40hp, and four-speed transmission.

Perhaps the ultimate Dauphine was the 1093 introduced in 1962. Only about 1,000 were made. With dual Solex carburetors, 9.2:1 compression ratio, hot camshaft, Gordini cylinder head, and domed pistons, the 845cc engine produced 55hp at 5600rpm. A beefed-up clutch and gearbox were used to handle the additional power. Externally, the 1093s were painted white, displayed "1093" decals, and had two narrow blue racing stripes running over the center of the car from front to rear.

The Dauphine was extremely popular and was the first French car to go over the two million unit mark. Dauphines were also built by Alfa Romeo in Italy and Willys-Overland in Brazil.

1959-68 Renault Floride and Caravelle

Like the VW with its Karmann-Ghia, Renault offered a sporty version of the Dauphine. Also like VW, Renault turned to Italians for design (the Ghia part) and an independent body builder (the Karmann part). Allemano of Italy designed the attractive body, and Brissoneau and Lotz did the final assembly in France.

It first appeared in 1959 as the Floride. For the American market, the name was changed to Caravelle. The Floride and Caravelle came in three forms—a convertible, with a removable hardtop, and a 2+2 hardtop coupe. The coupe had a longer, more squared-off top for a bit more headroom. The Caravelles used Dauphine running gear, underpan, suspension, and had an 89in wheelbase. With an overall length of 167.7in, there was much overhang in front and rear. The weight distribution, due to the rear-mounted engine, lead to noticeable oversteer, but the rather large front trunk could be loaded to improve things a bit.

The early Florides used a 40hp version of the Dauphine engine. The added power came from a hotter cam, slightly higher compression ratio, and a larger carburetor. Top speed was a mere 75mph. A three- or four-speed manual transmission and the Ferlec semi-automatic transmission were available.

When the Caravelle appeared in 1962, it was given a new engine from the Renault R8 with a displacement of 956cc and 51hp. By

The Caravelle was a direct competitor to the Volkswagen Karmann-Ghia. Like the K-G, this was a sporty car, rather than a true sports car. *Renault*

1964, this engine was rebored for 1108cc and between 55 and 58hp, depending on the year. Now the car could hit 90mph. Four-wheel disc brakes were standard. In all, some 117,000 Florides and Caravelles were built.

1961-89 Renault R4/R4L

The 4CV was replaced by another back-to-basics car, the R4, in 1961. It was no secret that the R4 was aimed at giving the Citroen 2CV some competition. Like the 2CV, the R4 had front-wheel-drive. Renault used the 4CV's 747cc engine in the R4. The station wagon-like R4 provided seating for four. In later years, the engine was upgraded to the 845cc engine from the Dauphine.

1962-72 R8, R8 Major, and R8 Gordini

The R8 replaced the Dauphine. While still using the 89in wheelbase and at 157in only 2in longer, the boxier R8 was roomier. Until 1964, the R8 used the 956cc engine from the Caravelle. In the R8, the engine produced 48hp. In 1964, R8s with the four-speed manuals got a 1108cc, 51hp engine. This version was called the R8 Major in many markets. Automatic versions continued to use the smaller engine. Four-wheel disc brakes were used, and you could order the R8, as well as Caravelles and even Dauphines, with air conditioning. When the last R8 left the factory in 1972, it was Renault's last rear-engined car. A Gordini version of the R8 was offered between 1965 and 1970 with the 1108cc unit fitted with twin

Solex carburetors and a 10.5:1 compression ratio to produce 95hp. There was also a heavy-duty suspension and a tachometer. This was superseded in 1967 by a Gordini version with a 1289cc engine.

1972-84 Renault 5 and Le Car

The Renault 5, sold as the Le Car in the United States after 1977, was a huge success. When replaced by the Supercinq in 1985, Renault had produced over 5.4 million, including cars produced in several locations outside of France. Through the years, the R5 was fitted with a wide variety of front-mounted, four-cylinder engines, including displacements of 845cc, 956cc, 1289cc, and an Alpine-tuned 1397cc. Hardly a minicar, except in size, was the Renault 5 Turbo with its 160hp obtained via turbocharging and fuel injection of the 1397cc engine mounted in the rear. The latter was easily distinguished by its huge wheel flares.

The R5's modern, fully independent suspension system used unequal-length arms with torsion bars. In the rear there were trailing arms and torsion bars. Interestingly, though not surprising for a French design, the R5 had two different wheelbases. It was 94.5in on one side and 95.8in on the other. Overall, the R5 was a rather short 142.5in.

Simca

Societe Industrielle de Mecanique et de Carrosserie Automobile, or Simca, was founded in 1934 to build Fiats under license. Until the 1951 Simca Aronde, Simcas were badge-engineered Fiats. Chrysler obtained a 15 percent share of Simca in 1958, which increased to about two-thirds by 1963, and by 1967 owned most of the French company. The name was changed to Chrysler France SA in 1970. In 1978, Chrysler sold out to Peugeot-Citroen.

The R8 was the Dauphine's replacement. This 1965 model, owned by Ronald Eppley, has traveled less than 120 miles. *Ronald Eppley*

'36-47 Cinq 2-door coupe	★★★★
'48-51 Six 2-door coupe	★★★★
'61-78 1000 4-door sedan	★★
'62-67 Bertone 2-door coupe	★★★★
'63 Simca Abarth 1150	★★★

The front-wheel-drive Renault 4/4L replaced the 4CV and was in production for nearly three decades. *Renault*

1936-51 Simca Cinq and Six

Simca's biggest seller before World War II was the Simca Cinq (Five), the French version of the Fiat 500. Like the Topolino, the Cinq used the 570cc, four-cylinder engine. Italian-born "tuner" Amedee Gordini, who greatly enhanced the Simca image through success in motorsports, was able to eke out an amazing 28hp from the engine for competition cars. Starting in 1939, the Simca Cinq was built completely in France. After World War II, production of the Cinq resumed with little change and continued until 1948 when it was replaced by the Simca Six. Like the updated Fiat 500C, styling was modernized with a new grille and front end featuring headlights integrated into the fenders. The two were now different enough that it was easy to distinguish between the Fiat 500C and Simca Six. Like the Fiat version, the Six used a new ohv, 570cc engine rated at 16hp.

1961-78 Simca 1000

Simca's most successful postwar model was the 1000, designed to compete against the Renault Dauphine, Citroen Ami 6, and so forth. Within a year of introduction, the 1000 was the best selling car in France, and by 1966, production had exceeded the one million mark. Since Fiat still had a major stake in Simca, the 1000 was derived from the Fiat 122, a design abandoned by Fiat.

The "1000" designation referred to the 944cc, four-cylinder, water-cooled engine located in the rear. Initially, the engine produced 35hp, then 44, and finally 55. The floor-shifted, four-speed transaxle was fully synchronized, and a three-speed, semi-automatic transmission became optional in 1966. The fully independent suspension system used upper control arms with transverse leaf springs in front and trailing swing arms and coil springs in the rear. The unitized body was 149in long and rode on an 87in wheelbase. Besides the four-door sedan, there was also a rather handsome sport coupe that used a body supplied by Bertone that was available between 1962 and 1967. Other specs included four-wheel drum brakes (disc/drum on the coupe) and Gemmer cam-and-roller steering. Simca 1000s were sold in the United States starting in 1963 and after 1967 wore a Chrysler Pentastar logo.

In 1963, Simca called upon Carlo Abarth to improve the 1000's image a bit. The result was the Simca-Abarth 1150 with the 944cc engine increased to 1137cc. Output was 55hp in the Simca-Abarth Berlina, 58 or 65 in the "S" version, and 85hp in the rare Corsa version. Other changes included Abarth wheels, steering wheel, and a front-mounted radiator. The Simca-Abarth was not particularly successful. A far better product of Abarth's involvement was the 1962-65 Abarth 1300/1600/2000 series that was more loosely based on the 1000 platform.

Vespa

Some ten million Vespa motorscooters have been built to date, making it the most prolific motorscooter brand in the world. In many places "Vespa" and "motorscooter" are synonymous. Aircraft builder Piaggo got into motorscooters and sewing machines, two items in demand in post-World War II

Italy. The scooter with its bulbous front and rear ends joined by a slim waistline was very wasplike; therefore the name Vespa, or wasp in Italian.

1958-61 Vespa 400

In the mid-1950s, Piaggo decided to get into the automobile business. The Vespa 400 had a wheelbase of only 66.7in and an overall length of only 112in, about a foot shorter than the petite Fiat 500 Topolino. This was a two-seater with room behind the seat for some cargo, small children, or an adult in a pinch. There was no front trunk on this rear-engined car, just a drawer-like compartment in lieu of a grille that held the battery and allowed access to the master cylinder mounted on the side. The spare tire rode under the passenger seat.

The Vespa was powered by a two-cylinder, two-stroke, air-cooled engine with a displacement of 393cc. With a peak horsepower of 20 at 4600rpm, it could push the 750lb car up to about 56mph. Fuel economy of 60mpg was claimed. There was a three-speed, floor-shifted, synchromesh transmission (some later cars had four speeds), drum brakes, and rack and pinion steering. The fully independent suspension system used deep-coil springs in front and a swing axle in the rear. The Vespa rode on tiny 4.40x10 tires. Handling was reportedly sports car-like. Indeed, Vespa did well in rallies, including the Rallye de Monte Carlo, often winning in the 500cc and sometimes the 750cc classes.

Rather than building the Vespa in Italy, production was assigned to Ateliers de Constructions de Motos et Accessories (ACMA) in France. ACMA built Vespa scooters under license. Reportedly, Piaggo felt that the Fiat Nuova 500 had the Italian minicar market pretty well sewed up. The Vespa could be licensed in the 2CV tax category in France. A few thousand Vespa 400s were sold in the United States in the late 1950s and early 1960s. These Vespas sold for $1,080, about $500 less than a Volkswagen

While called a convertible, the Vespa 400 was really a two-door coupe with a plastic fabric sunroof that rolled down to the rear deck. This handsome Vespa belongs to Rich Bachmann. *Rich Bachmann*

Beetle. The well-engineered car sold relatively well throughout the world, to the tune of about 28,000 units. Even so, Piaggo canceled production in 1961 to concentrate on motorscooters and aircraft.

Chapter 3

Germany

Minicars and microcars were especially popular as Germany got back on its feet after World War II. For manufacturers like Messerschmitt and Heinkel, microcars were the means to transition from war to peace products. Many of the German small cars were directly tied to Germany's highly advanced motorcycle industry. Motorcycle manufacturers like BMW, DKW, Zundapp, and NSU all offered microcars. As might be expected from a country noted for its engineering, many small German cars were highly innovative.

The first car to wear the BMW roundel was the Dixi 3/15, just a British Austin Seven built under license. BMW, which built aircraft engines starting in 1916, then motorcycles after World War I, inherited the 3/15 with its 15hp, 748.5cc, four-cylinder engine when it acquired *Fahrzeugfabrik Eisenbach* Eisenach Vehicle Factory in 1928. *BMW NA*

BMW

The first car to wear the BMW roundel was the tiny Dixi 3/15, which was just a British Austin Seven. BMW's first products were aircraft engines, and after World War I, motorcycles. It became an auto maker by acquiring the Fahrzeugfabrik Eisenbach in 1928, inheriting the Dixi.

Heavily damaged by allied bombing, BMW did not produce its first postwar cars until 1952, the six-cylinder "Baroque Angels." Hardly the right cars for the austere conditions, BMW was soon building a more appropriate vehicle, the Isetta.

'55-62 Isetta 250	★★★
'56-62 Isetta 300	★★★
'56-62 Isetta Cabrio	★★★★
'57-59 600 2-door	★★★

1955-62 BMW Isetta 250 and 300

The Isetta story starts in Italy with Renzo Rivolta and son Piero who operated Iso Automotovielto SpA in Milan. Between 1948 and 1960, it was one of Italy's major motorscooter makers. The Iso or "little Iso," debuting in 1953, resulted when the Rivoltas wanted a vehicle with more protection than a motorscooter without sacrificing much economy.

The Iso-Isetta used a 236cc, two-cylinder, two-stroke, 8hp engine. The engine was a "twingle," because the twin-cylinders used a common combustion chamber, intake port

The Iso-Isetta looks identical to the BMW Isetta. However, they differ in the details to the point that none of the parts are interchangeable. This beautiful Iso-Isetta was restored by Paul Bates. *Paul Bates*

In 1956, the BMW Isetta was revised with two-section sliding glass side windows for better ventilation and a smaller rear window. Cargo capacity was still limited to a pizza box-sized parcel shelf behind the seat. *Bill Siuru*

and exhaust port, and spark plug. Offered between 1953 and 1956 in Italy, the Iso-Isetta did not sell exceptionally well. The Rivoltas sold the rights to BMW. Iso also licensed the design to Romi-Isetta in Brazil and VELAM Isetta in France. Right-hand-drive, three-wheel versions were built by Isetta Great Britain, Ltd., between 1957 and

The original BMW Isetta design had a canvas roof, wraparound rear window, nonopening side windows, and triangular front vent windows. This outstanding Isetta 300 is owned by Marilyn Felling. *A. Meyer*

The first generation BMW Isetta Cabrio had a "Targa" top with a folding rear window unit, plus a steel roof panel and foldback sunroof. The cabriolet offered in the second series body style was essentially a normal Isetta with an oversized sunroof. This perfectly restored Isetta 300 Cabrio is owned by George Regalo. *George Regalo*

Iso also produced Isothermos refrigerators. Could this have influenced the design of the Isetta's single door? The Isetta's steering wheel and instrument panel moved with the door for easier access. The gearshift stalk on the side wheel well used a somewhat confusing reverse "H" pattern. *George Regalo*

1964. Limited numbers were also produced in Australia, Belgium, Spain, and Venezuela.

While using the Iso-Isetta design, the "das rollende Ei" (the rolling egg) was revised and improved by BMW. BMW used a motorcycle-based 247cc, four-stroke, air-cooled single-cylinder engine that produced 12hp. It was matched up to a four-speed manual transmission. The entire drivetrain was placed ahead of narrowly spaced rear wheels—20.5in compared to 47.2in for the front wheels—eliminating the need for a conventional differential.

The Isetta 300 referred to the 298cc engine which was used in both body styles. Horsepower was 13 at 5200rpm. Both 250 and 300 versions had a top speed in the range of 50 to 55mph, 40 to 45mpg in city driving, and over 50mpg on the highway.

The Isetta's suspension used leading swing arms and coil springs up front and a live rear axle with quarter-elliptic leaf springs. Early cars had friction shocks that were replaced by hydraulic ones. Drum brakes and 4.80x10 tires were used. The initial design had a 58in wheelbase and was only 90in long. With the body redesign, the wheelbase grew to 59.1in and overall length was 92.7in.

BMW sold 74,312 Isetta 250s and 84,416 Isetta 300s. Isettas, mostly 300s, started appearing in the United States in 1957 with a price tag of $1,048. Cars for the American market included a sunroof and a heater. They also got larger 7in sealed beam headlamps, additional taillights with turn signals, and heavier steel tube bumpers. About 8,500 Isettas were sold to Americans.

The Iso design was also adapted for trucks, going under names like Isocarro, Isettacarro, and Autocarro. They required some major modifications such as rear frames, normally spaced rear wheels, and elliptic leaf spring suspension. Since the engine remained behind the rear seat, a drive shaft and differential had to be used. *Paul Bates*

1957-59 BMW 600

The BMW 600 was a four-seat alternative to the Isetta. It had an additional door on the right-side and an another cylinder in the engine. The 600 had a 66.9in wheelbase and overall length of 114.2in. Power came from a twin-cylinder, four-stroke, air-cooled, 582cc engine like BMW's famous flat-twin motorcycle powerplant and was rated at 26hp. The fully synchronized four-speed transmission was now shifted via a conventional floor-mounted gearshift. Top speed for the 600 was about 65mph, and 60mpg, was claimed. The 600's *Schraglenker-Hinterache* semi-trailing arm, independent rear suspension system is still used in BMWs, albeit with many significant improvements. Some 34,813 BMW 600s were sold.

1959-65 BMW 700

BMW 700 underpinnings can be traced to the 600. The BMW 700 used a rear-mounted engine similar to the 600's but increased to 697cc and initially rated at 30hp. The 700 also had the 600's independent rear suspension system. Up front, the independent front suspension used upper and lower trailing arms with coil springs. The BMW 700 was fitted with a four-speed manual transmission with rubber bushings, resulting in a somewhat mushy feel. The rack and pinion steering was quite precise, and there were very efficient 8in drum brakes all around. 700s were fitted with 12in wheels.

BMW proudly displayed its familiar roundel logo on several locations on the BMW 600. The nerf bars were used on BMW Isettas and 600s for a bit more protection. *A. Meyer*

'59-62 700 2-door sedan	★★
'59-64 700 2-door coupe	★★★
'60-64 700 Sport/CS coupe	★★★★
'63-64 700 convertible	★★★★★
'62-65 700 LS 2-door sedan	★★
'64-65 700 LS coupe	★★★★

The BMW 700 Sport was introduced in 1962. The main difference being 40hp obtained via dual Solex 34 PCI carburetors versus the single Solex on the standard 700s, a 9:1 compression ratio versus the standard 7.5:1, larger intake valves, and a more radical camshaft. Regular 700s got a power boost to 32hp for 1962. The 700 Sport, which was retitled the CS (Coupe Sport) for 1963-64, also got a rear antiroll bar.

In 1962, BMW offered the stretched BMW 700 LS sedan with an 89.8in wheelbase and an overall length of 152in, up from 139.4in for the rest of the 700s. Most of the stretch went into extra space for the rear passengers. Even though the LS had more rear overhang, it was of little use since BMW

Giovanni Michelotti styled the 700's attractive body. The first 700s rode on an 83.5in wheelbase and were the first BMWs to use unit construction. *BMW AG*

did not want to further disturb the car's strong rear weight bias by hanging more weight at the tail. The stretched 700 was available first only in Luxus form; then in 1963, a lower-priced LS version appeared. Of all the 700s, the rarest is the 700 LS coupe that appeared in 1965, but unlike the sedan, it was powered by the 40hp Sport engine. The LS coupe provided more rear seat room over the smaller coupes, which were noted for their ultra thin front seats, to give 2+2 seating.

The 700 sedans bore signs of BMW styling that would later appear on the BMW 1602 and 2002 sedans. The engine was still in the rear, so there was no BMW kidney-shaped grille, just small, fake horn grilles on either side of the headlights. This 1963 BMW 700 Luxus sedan is owned by Edwina DeRousse. *Paul DeRousse*

BMW 700 Cabriolets were produced by coach-builder Baur. This one is owned by Bill and Starr Young. *Bill Siuru*

DKW

By 1927, DKW was the world's largest motorcycle manufacturer, a title held until the start of World War II, marketing them as the Das Kleine Wunder (The Little Wonder). The Zschopauer Motoren-Werke J. S. Rasmussen AG, as the company was then known, produced the first DKW car in 1928. It used a two-stroke, two-cylinder, water-cooled engine with a displacement of 494cc, which grew to 584cc. DKW was the first to successfully use two-strokes in cars. The first DKWs were chassisless with wooden construction. Front-wheel drive, another DKW hallmark, debuted in 1931 and was called "DKW-Front." The DKW F1 and F2 were the world's first mass-produced front-wheel-drive cars. They were designed by Audi since DKW, Audi, Horch, and Wanderer all became part of Auto Union AG in 1932. The F1 had a 490cc engine, whereas the F2 used a 584cc unit. By the mid-1930s, only Opel produced more cars in Germany. Popular prewar DKW models included the two-cylinder, front-wheel-drive 584cc Reichklasse and 684cc Meisterklasse. Dividing up Germany after World War II resulted in Auto Union AG having no factories in the western zones. Auto Union employees set up a central parts depot to keep some 60,000 wooden-bodied prewar DKWs running. By 1949, Auto Union was not only producing spare parts but also DKW RT 125 motorcycles and DKW F89 L delivery vans.

1950-54 Meisterklasse

The first postwar model was the 1950 Meisterklasse using the mechanics of the prewar Meisterklasse with a new body based on a 1940 F9 prototype. The Meisterklasse had a two-cylinder, two-stroke, 23hp, 684cc engine. Some 70,900 had been built when production ceased in 1954. Most desirable are the two-seat coupe and cabriolet, built by Hebmueller, and the Karmann-built four-seat cabriolet.

'50-52 2-door coupe	★★★★
'50-54 2-door limousine (sedan)	★★★
'50-54 2-door cabriolet	★★★★★
'50-54 2-door (Universal) station wagon	★★★

1953-59 Sonderklasse 3=6

DKW put the three-cylinder prewar F9 prototype into production as the Sonderklasse. The series was also called the 3=6. DKW claimed the 896cc, three-cylinder, two-stroke performed like a six-cylinder four-stroke. Since a two-stroke produces power on every piston stroke, the popcorn popper engine turned into a rather smooth runner when the revs were up. DKW sold some 232,148 of the 3=6s between 1953 and

'53-'59 2-door coupe	★★★★
'53-'59 2-door sedan	★★★
'55-'59 4-door sedan	★★★
'55-'59 2-door hardtop coupe	★★★★
'53-'59 2-door station wagon	★★★
'53-'57 2-door, 4-pass. convertible	★★★★★
'53-'57 2-door, 2-pass. convertible	★★★★★
'56-'68 Munga 4WD	★★★
'53-'59 Panel truck or minibus	★★★
'57-'58 Monza sport coupe	★★★★★

The DKW engine was a model of simplicity, running without valves, camshaft, lifters, pushrods, and rocker arms. The thermosyphon cooling system did away with the need for a water pump. Oil was added to the gasoline, eliminating the complexity of an oil pump and sump. The engine was placed well ahead of the front axle. The four-speed transaxle was located behind the engine. The radiator was located above and behind the engine. *Audi*

Though this is a two-door sedan, DKW was one of the first European auto makers to offer a hardtop coupe. The suicide doors, a throwback to prewar designs, were replaced in 1958, but only on two-door models. *Audi*

1959. DKW 3=6s started appearing in the United States in 1955.

Initially, the 896cc engine produced 38hp. This was upped to 42hp in 1955 and 45hp in 1958. DKWs featured freewheeling which was operated by a lever under the dashboard. Early 3=6s had a three-speed with overdrive gearbox, which was soon replaced by a four-speed. Both used a column shift with an unusual shift pattern. A semi-

The DKW four-door sedan and two-door Universal station wagon were a bit longer with a 96.5in wheelbase. *Audi*

In an attempt to update a basic design that was now over twenty years old, the Auto-Union hardtop had a wraparound windshield. This 1960 Auto Union 1000S is owned by Craig Vigle. *Jim Craig*

The 1957-58 Monza coupe used a fiberglass body on DKW 3=6 mechanics. Monzas set five world records on their namesake track. *Otto Hoffmann*

automatic Saxomat transmission was optional. The rather rare cabriolets with padded tops were built by Karmann. DKW van-like trucks came in pickup, panel, and eight-passenger minibus versions.

DKW also offered a two-seat, fiberglass-bodied sport coupe based on the 3=6 chassis called the Monza. While some sources claim that 110 to 170 examples were built, Auto Union records indicate that only fifty-three chassis were delivered to Dannenhauser-and-Stauss and Fritz Wenk, two companies that built the Monza. Early examples were powered by the 38hp, 896cc engine. Later ones featured the 50hp, 980cc engine or the 62hp 980cc engine used in the Auto Union 1000SP.

Other specialty coachbuilders used the DKW chassis. One was the DKW Spyder, built in small numbers by Wendler in the mid-1950s. The Spyder's aluminum body was about 300lb lighter than a stock 1956 DKW sedan, but it cost a whopping $5,600 delivered in Los Angeles.

1958-62 Auto Union 1000

In 1958, the Auto Union 1000 was introduced with a 980cc, 50hp, three-cylinder engine or 57hp in the 1000S versions. Outside of the bigger engine, the Auto Union 1000s were just badge-engineered DKWs with trim changes such as elimination of the 3=6's ribs on the trunk lid and installation of Auto-Union's four interlinked circles logo.

'58-65 2-door sedan	★★★
'60-65 4-door sedan	★★★
'68-65 2-door hardtop coupe	★★★
'60-65 2-door station wagon	★★★
'58-65 1000SP sport coupe	★★★★★
'61-65 1000SP roadster	★★★★★
add one-half star for 1000S versions	

While using Auto-Union 1000-series mechanics, the 1000SP coupe and convertible had a completely different body done by Baur. It looked a bit like a shrunken 1955 Ford Thunderbird. *Otto Hoffmann*

47

The DKW Lived On and On and On!

While the West German auto industry flourished, East German cars were a visible testimony to the failure of Communism. When production of Trabants and Wartburgs ceased in the early 1990s, they were still largely based on prewar DKW technology. Much of what was left of DKW wound up on the wrong side of the Iron Curtain and part of *Industrie-Veriningung Volkseigner Fahrzeugwerke* (IFA). This was a nationalized conglomerate of several prewar German auto makers including DKW and Audi.

The first product was the 1948-55 IFA F8, just the prewar DKW Meisterklasse with its two-cylinder, two-stroke, 684cc engine, front-wheel drive, and prewar body styling that was built at the former Audi factory in Zwickau. In 1950, the F8 was joined by the IFA F9 based on the prewar DKW F9 prototype which was not produced before the war. The F9 featured a three-cylinder, two-stroke, 894cc engine and new body styling. Initially produced at Zwickau, production was moved to VEB Automobilwerke Eisenach which used the former BMW facilities in Eisenach.

Millions of "plastic" Trabant 601s were seen on the roads of former East Germany; most were driven at their top speed—62mph. *Bill Siuru*

The Zwickau P70 replaced the F8 in 1956 and was now produced by VEB Automobilwerke Zwickau. The P70 used the 684cc engine and IFA F8 running gear, but with a fiberglass body. In 1959, the P70 became the Trabant P50 with the two-stroke, two-cylinder engine downsized to 500cc. Trabant means "fel-

This restored IFA F9 was spotted in East Berlin shortly after the wall came down. *Bill Siuru*

The Trabant Tramp "sport utility" was commonly used by the East German "Polizei." *Bill Siuru*

The most desirable Auto Union 1000 models are the 1000SP coupe and rare companion convertible. The 980cc two-stroke produced 62hp. About 5,000 coupes were built, plus another 1,640 roadsters. Unfortunately, like all 3=6 and 1000 series DKWs, the 1000SP was fitted with an unsportscarlike column shifter for the four-speed.

1959-65 DKW 750, Junior, F11, F12, and F102

The DKW 750's 741cc, three-cylinder enlow traveler" in German, equivalent to the Russian "Sputnik." Early models used resin-re-inforced papier mache bodies because of shortages of fiberglass. In 1962, the P50's engine was increased to 594cc, and the designation was changed to the Trabant 600.

The Trabant 601 appeared in 1964, and there was also a two-door Universal Estate station wagon. In an attempt to bring the two-stroke engine into the 1980s, electronic fuel injection was used starting in 1985. About three million Trabants were built until 1992.

By 1956, the IFA F9 was replaced by the Wartburg 311. Wartburg was a brand built in Eisenach before BMW took over in 1928. The 311 was still powered by an 894cc, three-cylinder, two-stroke engine but carried a completely new body that, at least by East German standards, was mildly attractive. There was even a rather good-looking Model 313 coupe and sport roadster, plus a four-door station wagon. Engine capacity was increased to 991cc and 45hp in 1962.

The contemporary-looking Wartburg 353 went into production in 1966 and stayed in production through 1992, initially with the 311

powerplant. Because of its DKW heritage, the Wartburgs featured front-wheel drive. Wartburg 353s were marketed in several Western European countries. Their biggest attraction was their low price.

DKWs were also produced in Switzerland, between 1934 and 1939, as the Holka-DKW and in Sweden, immediately after World War II, as the Philipson-DKW. The DKW design more or less influenced the post-1955 Polish Syrena, the Argentine 1954-55 Justicialista, and its reincarnation, the 1960-61 Graciela.

Automoviles Eugenio Cortes SA in Barcelona, Spain, produced over 1,500 of its Eucort models between 1945 and 1949. The Eucorts used DKW mechanics including two-stroke, two-cylinder or three-cylinder engines. However, bodies were of Spanish design and included four-door sedans, convertibles, station wagons, and taxis. Some 115,000 Auto Union 1000 vehicles were built under license by DKW-Vemag in Brazil and Argentina between 1961 and 1967.

The Wartburg 313 was mildly attractive. The model included a cabriolet and coupe. Under the hood was a three-cylinder, two-stroke engine. *Bill Siuru*

After the fall of East Germany, the fourteen-year waiting list for a Wartburg 353, available after 1988 with a 1.3ltr Volkswagen four-cylinder engine, changed to long lines of unwanted cars. *Bill Siuru*

gine produced 39hp. The 750's styling was quite modern and American-looking, including headlight eyebrows and tiny tailfins. It still used body-frame construction when unit-body construction was common, especially on small cars.

The 750 had an 85.6in wheelbase and an overall length of 166in. The suspension used torsion bars up front and a rigid rear axle with laminated transverse torsion bars, trailing arms, and a track rod. Drum brakes were still used all around with the front brakes lo-

The DKW F12 convertible's engine produced 50hp at 4500rpm, reportedly achieved by installing a larger carburetor on individual engines that produced output power at the high end of the power band on the test stand. The F12 convertible also used inboard-mounted disc brakes up front. *Otto Hoffmann*

cated inboard. The shifter for the four-speed transmission was still on the steering column.

By 1962, all DKWs used an automatic oil feed system that eliminated the need to pre-mix oil and gasoline. The automatic system injected oil at the carburetor. However, thermosyphon cooling was used on DKWs to the very end. The 1962-63 Junior was essentially the 750 fitted with a 796cc engine, but horsepower remained at 39, though torque increased a bit.

The F11 had a 796cc, 39hp, three-cylinder engine while the F12 had an 889cc engine that rated at 45hp. The F11 and F12 sedans stuck with drum brakes. Almost 351,000 750s, Juniors, F11s, and F12s were built.

By 1958, Auto-Union was acquired by Daimler-Benz. In 1965, Volkswagen bought Auto-Union and within a year the DKW was dropped in favor of Audi. Indeed, the F102, the successor to the 3=6 and Auto Union 1000 appearing in 1964, would become the first postwar Audi. The F102, the last DKW two-stroke, used a three-cylinder, 1175cc engine. Even though two-strokes were rapidly falling out of favor, 53,053 F102s were sold.

'60-61 750 2-door sedan	★★
'62-63 Junior 2-door sedan	★★
'63-65 F11 2-door sedan	★★
'63-65 F12 2-door sedan	★★
'63-65 F12 2-door convertible	★★★★
'64-66 F102 2-door sedan	★★

The Munga was a four-wheel-drive vehicle based on the DKW 3=6. Introduced in 1956 and produced until 1968, it the last vehicle to use the DKW three-cylinder engine. Some 46,750 Mungas were produced for military and civilian use. *Audi*

The DKW 750, Junior, F11, and F12 (shown here) were good-selling alternatives to the VW Beetle. The F12 was built on a 3in longer 88.6in wheelbase. *Audi*

Glas

Hans Glas GmbH was already a mature manufacturer when it got into the automotive business in the mid-1950s. The nameplate disappeared shortly after BMW bought financially troubled Glas in 1966.

1955-69 Goggomobil

Compared to other German microcars such as the Isetta, Heinkel, and Messerschmitt, the Goggomobil was pretty conventional. The first ten prototypes built in late 1954 did have a single front door, but was soon changed to more conventional side doors. The front trunk was accessed from the front passenger footwell as there was no opening up front. While only 114in long with a 71in wheelbase, the Goggomobil was touted as a four-passenger car. A fabric sunroof model, sometimes called the Hollywood, was optional.

'55-69 T250 2-door sedan	★★★
'55-65 T300 2-door sedan	★★★
'57-67 T400 2-door sedan	★★★
'57-65 TS250 2-door coupe	★★★★
'57-69 TS300 2-door coupe	★★★
'57-68 TS400 2-door coupe	★★★
'57-65 TC250/300 convertible	★★★★★
'57-65 TL250/300/400 Transporter pickups and vans	★★★

Goggomobils were powered by rear-mounted, motorcycle-type, two-cylinder, air-cooled engines driving the rear wheels. The engines came in three sizes—247cc with 13.6hp in the 250, 296cc with 14.8hp in the 300, and 18 to 20hp in the 400. Depending on the engine, top speeds ranged from 53 to 62mph. Likewise, fuel economy ranged from 40 to 80mpg. The T400 was even raced, taking home several class wins.

The four-speed transaxle was integrated with the engine. There was an optional Getrag Electro-magnetic Gearbox where gears were selected by a 2in selector lever protruding from the instrument panel. The shift was made when the clutch pedal was pushed in. There was a separate button for reverse.

The designers did a good job in styling the Goggomobil coupe, considering its overall length was only 119.5in, about 5in longer than the sedan. Like the sedan, there were suicide doors, and coupes usually came in bright two-tone colors with a more upscale interior. The TS400 also carried the name deVille, and there was a rare TC250/300 convertible.

The 296cc sedan and coupe were titled the Regent T300 and Mayfair TS300, respectively, in 1957, first for the British market,

The Goggomobil's rear-hinged doors were replaced by front-hinged ones in 1964 in response to new German laws that prohibited suicide doors. Prior to the fall of 1956, sliding windows were used; then wind-up windows were used. This is a T250. *Automuseum Story*

With its heart-shaped grille, the Goggomobil coupe looked vaguely like a miniature Alfa-Romeo. The coupe was optimistically called a four-passenger vehicle, though the rear seat was tight, even for children. *Kazmier Wysocki*

then in other English-speaking markets. The Goggomobil was also built in pickup and van form with all three engine sizes used. The forward control, 1/4-ton, step-in TL400 minivan was widely used by the German postal service.

The Goggomobiles had a four-wheel independent suspension system easily recognized by the canted 4.40x10 tires (4.80x10 on the coupe). Up front, there were swinging semi-axles, coil springs, and telescopic shocks. Swinging axles, oblique trailing radius arms, coil springs, and telescopic shocks were used in the rear. The unibody used a press steel platform with a central tube and diagonal ribs.

The Goggomobile was Glas' longest running and most profitable model. A total of 214,313 sedans and 66,511 coupes were produced between 1955 and 1969. Some 6100 Goggomobiles were produced by Munguia Industrial Spain. Goggomobils were assembled in Australia from components by the Buckle Organization, which also built a couple of unique models with fiberglass bodies—a cabriolet and a two-seat "sports car," known as the Goggomobil Dart.

1957-66 Isar T600 and T700

By 1957, Glas was also producing a slightly larger car, the Isar T600, still using an air-cooled, two-cylinder engine. However, the 584cc, 19hp engine was now a four-stroke and was located up front driving the rear wheels. A more "potent" Isar T700 later appeared with the engine uprated to 688cc and 30hp. Top speed was around 60mph for the T600 and 70mph for the T700. The styling included an American-style wrap-around windshield and Buick-like sweepspear side trim. A T700 kombi appeared in 1959. Nearly 87,000 Isars had been built before production ceased in 1965.

'57-65 T600 2-door sedan	★★
'58-65 T700 2-door sedan	★★
'59-65 T700 2-door kombi	★★

The T600/T700 used an independent front suspension system that included trailing upper wishbones and transverse lower arms

in conjunction with coil springs and telescopic dampers. The rear had a live axle mounted via semi-elliptic leaf springs. Steering was cam-and-peg and drum brakes were used all around.

1962-66 1004

In 1962, Glas brought out the larger car 1004 with a 992cc overhead-cam, four-stroke, four-cylinder, water-cooled powerplant that cranked out 42hp. This engine pioneered a camshaft that was driven by a tooth belt rather than a chain, a feature that would be used by many automakers. The four-speed transmission was fully synchromesh. The front-mounted engine drove the rear wheels. The 1004 was offered as a two-door sedan, 2+2 coupe, convertible, and kombi station wagon. TS versions were available with a 64hp engine. The basic engine later grew to 53hp and 70hp in the TS version. Body and chassis were combined with a 1189cc engine in 1204 models and 1290cc in the 1304. The wheelbase was 83in, and the overall length measured 151in.

'63-67 Limousine 2-door sedan	★★
'65-67 Station wagon	★★
'62-67 2+2 coupe	★★★
'63-67 Cabriolet	★★★★

Goliath

Goliath-Werke GmbH was part of the Borgward Group, fitting between top-of-the-line Borgwards and the entry level Lloyd. Before World War II, Goliath built three-wheeled mini-trucks, but between 1931 and 1933, it did offer a three-wheel car called the Pionier. The Pionier featured a single-cylinder, two-stroke, 198cc Ilo engine driving the twin rear wheels.

1950-56 Goliath GP 700 and GP 900

The GP 700 two-door sedan had a two-stroke, two-cylinder, water-cooled 688cc engine that produced 22 to 26hp. Other features included a nonsynchronized four-speed transmission shifted via a dashboard-mounted gearshift lever, a central tube frame with a 90.6in wheelbase, and rack and pinion steering. The suspension used two transverse elliptic springs up front and longitudinal elliptic leaf springs in the rear.

'50-56 GP 700 2-door sedan	★★★
'50-56 GP 700 2-door Sport Coupe	★★★★★
'50-56 GP 900 2-door sedan	★★★
'57-61 1100 2-door sedan	★★★
'57-60 1100 2-door convertible	★★★★
'57-61 1100 2-door station wagon	★★★
'57-61 1100 Tiger 2-door coupe	★★★★
'57-61 1100 Empress 2-door sedan	★★★

Goliath and Gutbrod offered the first fuel-injection system used on a gasoline-engined production car. In 1951, the Goliath GP 700 and a new GP 900 were fuel-injected. The GP 900 used a two-cylinder, two-stroke, water-cooled, 886cc engine. With direct fuel injection, the 668cc engine produced 29hp, while the 886cc engine was rated at 40hp. These early fuel-injection systems were used to correct three shortcomings of two-stroke engines—poor fuel economy, excessive noise, and hard starting. With direct fuel injection, the injectors spray fuel directly into the combustion chamber.

The GP 900 two-door sedan was identical to the GP 700, except for the larger engine. More interesting was the GP 700 Sport Coupe. This fastback coupe with a body handcrafted by Rometsch of Berlin, looked a bit like the contemporary Porsche, except there was a grille for the front-mounted engine that drove the front wheels. Reportedly, only twenty-five Sport Coupes were built.

By 1957, Goliath was using a more conventional 1093cc, four-cylinder, four-stroke engine. The series was given the "1100" designation. A Solex carburetor replaced the fuel injection. The engine was horizontally opposed along the lines of the VW but was water-cooled. The engine was rated at 46hp, and the four-speed transmission was fully synchronized. By 1960, the dashboard-mounted gear selector was replaced by an equally imprecise column-mounted gearshift.

The handling of the 1100 was improved through the use of coil front springs in the place of the earlier transverse leaves. Besides a two-door sedan, there was also a convertible and station wagon. In 1958, two more

This brochure cover shows a Goliath GP 700 sedan. All Goliaths had front-wheel drive.

Even with the upgraded engine, the Goliath 1100 Tiger Sport Coupe was no hot rod. Contemporary road tests showed a 0 to 60mph time of 25 seconds and a top speed of 84mph. *Helmut Hubener*

models were added, the rather handsome Tiger two-passenger coupe and upscale Empress two-door sedan. The Tiger had an upgraded, twin-carbureted version of the engine that produced 63hp, versus a 46hp engine used in the other Goliath 1100s.

Gutbrod

1949-54 Gutbrod

Gutbrod-Motorenbau GmbH started producing cars in 1949 under the Gutbrod Superior label. Along with the Goliath, it was the first to feature fuel injection. Direct-injection FI was used on the 593cc Superior 600/604 and 663cc Superior 700/704.

'49-54 600/700 2-door coupe	★★★
'49-54 604/704 2-door station wagon	★★★
'49-54 600/700 roadster/convertible	★★★★

The car lived a bit longer after Gutbrod itself ceased production in 1954. Troll Plastik-og Bilindustri in Norway purchased surplus parts from Gutbrod and designed a rather attractive, fiberglass-bodied, two-seat, fastback coupe called the Troll. The Troll used the two-cylinder 663cc Gutbrod engine

Even though a small producer, Gutbrod offered a full range of models, including a two-door coupe, four-passenger sedan, and station wagons, convertibles, roadsters. minivans, kombis, and cab-chassis for special bodies.

and four-wheel independent suspension. Only five Trolls were built in 1956.

Heinkel

Ernest Heinkel AG produced some 170,000 motorscooters between 1953 and 1965. The Heinkel Kabine (Cabin) Cruiser that debuted in 1955 used the experience, technology, and even some of the componentry from these motorscooters. Heinkel's bubble car, with its huge windows all around, looked even more like a "rolling egg" than the BMW Isetta. Visibility from the Cabin Cruiser in all directions was almost as good as a convertible with the top down. The Heinkels also came with a rather large fabric sunroof, a necessity since only the smallish triangular front windows opened for ventilation. The Heinkel was advertized as being able to carry two adults and two children, but the latter had to climb over the front seats to get to the rear seats.

Initially, the Heinkel Type 407 B-0 and B-1 were three-wheelers with two wheels up front and one in the rear driven by an air-cooled, single-cylinder, four-stroke, 174cc, 9.2hp engine from the Heinkel Tourist 102 and 103 motorscooters. In late 1956, the engine was replaced by a 198cc for the Typ 408 B-2, with 10hp. About the same time, the three-wheeler was joined by a four-wheeler. The two rear wheels were only about 10in apart, still giving a three-wheel look.

Overall, the bubble car was 100in long (105 for the four-wheel version) and had a 69in wheelbase. It weighed 535 to 625lb. The motorscooter-type, four-speed gearbox was operated by a gated, quadrant gear changer. Hydraulic internally expanding brakes were used on the front wheels while there was a mechanical hand brake for the rear wheel or wheels. While the design appeared to be aerodynamically efficient, it was hardly necessary since the top speed was only about 55mph.

1955-65 Heinkel and Trojan

The Heinkel Cabin Cruiser was far less successful than the BMW Isetta, with only about 11,900 (6,400 three-wheelers and 5,500

Trojan '200'

TWO NEW MODELS

The Right Hand Drive Saloon

The Right Hand Drive Estate Van

The British Trojan 200 was virtually identical to the Heinkel Cabin Cruiser. Models included a saloon, estate wagon with a bit more cargo capacity, a light parcel van, and a rare convertible. Less than 7,000 Trojans were sold when production ceased in 1964.*Heinkel Trojan Owners and Enthusiasts Club*

four-wheelers) sold between 1955 and 1958. The Heinkel design was sold in 1958 to Dundalk Engineering in Ireland, which sold another 8,000 before selling the design to Trojan, Ltd., in England in 1960. The Trojan 200, with some changes and improvements, used right-hand drive and only three-wheels. Re-

The Trojan production line. Entry was through a single front door, but unlike the BMW Isetta, the steering wheel and instrument panel remained in place.*Heinkel Trojan Owners and Enthusiasts Club*

portedly, some 2,000 Heinkels were also made under license in Argentina between 1957 and 1959.

'55-58 Cabin Cruiser	★★★
'58-61 Heinkel-Ireland	★★★
'61-65 Trojan 200	★★★
add one star for convertible	

Lloyd

1950-57 LP 300, LP 400, and LP 600

The first postwar Lloyds were rather crude cars. The LP 300 used a motorcycle-like, two-cylinder, two-stroke, 293cc, 13hp engine. The body had a wooden frame covered with leatherette. Side windows slid open, the rear window was flat, and there was no external access to the small rear luggage compartment. Like all Lloyds, the LP 300 had front-wheel drive. The three-speed transmission was unsynchronized with a column-mounted gearshift. The LP 300 did have a fully independent suspension system and was only 137in long with a 78.7in wheelbase.

By 1953, the engine grew to 400cc for the

Early Lloyd 400 sedan with a leatherette over wood body. *John Lloyd*

LP 400. In addition to the two-door sedan, there was now a coupe and station wagon, or kombi. The body on all but the early LP 400s had steel doors, fenders, and so on, but

'50-52 LP 300 2-door sedan	★★
'53-54 LP 400 2-door sedan and kombi	★★
'53-54 LP 400 2-door coupe	★★★
'54-57 LP 600 2-door sedan and kombi	★★
'54-57 LP 600 2-door convertible	★★★★
TL 600 Minivan	★★
'57-61 Alexander (including TS) 2-door sedan and kombi	★★
'57-61 Alexander convertible	★★★★
'57-61 Alexander minivan	★★
'57-61 Arabella 2-door sedan	★★

The Lloyd Alexander with all-steel body and roll-up windows. *John Lloyd*

the roof and window frames were still wood. By 1954, all-steel bodies were used. In 1954, the twin-cylinder engine grew again to 597cc and 19hp for the LP 600, which now included a convertible where the side frames stayed in place when the top was rolled back. By 1955, the 100,000th Lloyd was built. Lloyds were exported to some seventy-two nations including the United States .

1957-61 Alexander and Alexander TS

While the basic rounded Lloyd body was retained for this new model, roll-up windows replaced sliding ones, and later models had modernized front-end styling. The engine was now four-stroke but still a two-cylinder. While the displacement was still 597cc, horsepower was increased to 24. There was also a proper trunk lid and a wraparound rear window on the sedan. A fully synchronized, four-speed transmission was initially offered as an option. A larger LT600 microbus was added to the line-up as well as an Alexander coupe designed by Frua of Italy. There was another horsepower increase to 29 with the 1959 TS or Touring Sport version of the Alexander. In 1959, the tiny Lloyd was the third best-selling marque in Germany.

1957-61 Arabella

The Arabella would be the last, and arguably the best, Lloyd. As the economic climate improved in Germany, Lloyd, like other automakers, began to offer cars that

The LT 600 microbus would not win any beauty contests. *John Lloyd*

provided more than just basic transportation. Besides being more stylish and a bit more luxurious, the Arabella featured a new 897cc, four-cylinder, horizontally-opposed engine that produced 34, 38, or 44hp. The manual four-speed, fully synchronized transmission still had a column shifter.

The Arabella had an 86.6in wheelbase and an overall length of 149.5in. The completely revised body styling included up-to-date items like finned rear fenders with canted taillights, slightly shrouded headlamps, and a wide mesh-patterned grille. Failure of Borgward in 1961 finished Lloyd, though a limited number were still built through 1963 from the leftover parts inventory.

Maico

1955-60 500, 500 Sport, and 700 Sport
Maico comes from Maich and Company, which started making motorcycles in the 1930s. After the war, Maico began making toys, then motorcycles, and upscale motorscooters, such as the Maico Mobil MB 150, MB 175, and MB 200.

In 1955, Maico began building cars when it acquired the designs for the Champion, another German microcar. The two-seat 1947-54 Champions used rear-mounted 250cc TWN, 400cc Ilo or 450cc Heinkel engines. The Champions found few buyers. The redesigned, rear-engined Maico 500, now a four-seater with suicide-type doors and sliding door windows, looked a bit like a Volkswagen Beetle. With a wheelbase of 79.5in and an overall length of 134.5in, it was considerably smaller. Early cars used a 398cc engine while later ones used a two-cylinder, two-stroke, water-cooled, 452cc engine that produced 18hp. The aluminum body was mounted on a central tube chassis.

The much better looking Maico 500 and 700 Sport two-passenger coupes looked quite like the contemporary Volkswagen Karmann Ghia. However, it was much smaller with a 79.5in wheelbase and an overall length of

134.5in. By 1958, cars were dropped, and the company concentrated on motorcycle production, though cars were sold as late as 1960.

Messerschmidt (Including Fend)
Contrary to common belief, famed aviation pioneer Willy Messerschmitt did not design the Messerschmitt Kabinenroller or cabin scooter. Credit for "inventing" the three-wheeler goes to Fritz Fend, who started out by building three-wheel scooters for invalids in the late 1940s. The first ones were manually operated, followed by versions powered by a 38cc Victoria, 98cc Sachs, or 100cc Reidel engine.

1950-53 Fend Flitzer
Next, Fend designed a two-place three-wheeler that established the basic design for the Kabinenroller. Powered by a two-stroke, single-cylinder engine, the Fend Flitzer used a unitized tubular frame covered by aluminum sheeting. While still aimed at the invalid market, the low price attracted buyers who wanted "wheels" but could not afford or even find a real car in postwar Germany. The Flitzer came either in open or closed form and about 250 were built.

1953-55 KR-175
As sales of Flitzer took off, Fend began looking for expanded manufacturing capacity. Willy Messerschmitt entered the picture as he was looking for a product to build at his plant, since he was forbidden to build aircraft. A deal was struck, with Fend responsible for development of the Kabinroller while Messerschmitt contributed only his name and facilities.

The FK-175, for Fend-Kabinenroller, had changed to the KR-175 when production started in 1953 and used a Fichtel and Sachs, air-cooled, two-stroke, single-cylinder 9hp engine. The engine drove the rear wheel via a motorcycle-type chain drive. A twist-grip

'55-60 500 2-door sedan	★★
'55-58 500 Sport 2-door coupe	★★★
'59-60 700 Sport 2-door coupe	★★★

'51-53 Fend Flitzer	★★★★★
'53-55 KR175	★★★
'55-64 KR200	★★★
'58-61 Tg500 Tiger	★★★★
add one-half star for open-top models	

The evolution of the Messerschmitt Kabinenroller. From right to left—Fend Flitzer, KR175, KR200, and Tg500. Contrary to folklore, the Messerschmitt was not designed to look like an aircraft, even though its three wheels were laid out like a "tail-dragger" and the two occupants were seated in tandem under a plexiglass bubble dome. *Automuseum Story*

throttle was located on the left side of the handlebar. To keep costs down, early models had a kick starter on the floor that was later replaced by an electric starter. The lack of a reverse gear required the driver to get out and push to back up.

The KR-175 was 111in long, had a 79.9in wheelbase, and weighed about 500lb. Tires were tiny 4.40x8s with a spare often mounted on the tail. The independent suspension system used soft rubber torsion springs, but there were no shock absorbers. Cable-operated mechanical drum brakes were fitted to all three wheels. Instrumentation was limited to a 100km/h speedometer, optional clock, a radio in the center, plus a few idiot lights and toggle switches.

1955-64 KR-200

An improved KR-200 began replacing the KR-175 in 1955. The 200 stood for the slightly larger, 191cc, 10.2hp Fichtel and Sachs engine. The extra horsepower did not change the bubble car's top speed of 62mph or its 50 to 70mpg fuel economy. The rubber torsion suspension was revised, and hydraulic shock absorbers were added. The front wheel track was increased from

The bubble-top on the KR200 was completely revised and featured a wraparound windshield; an electric windshield wiper replaced the manual one used on the KR-175. Wheel cutouts were added in the front fenders. *A. Meyer*

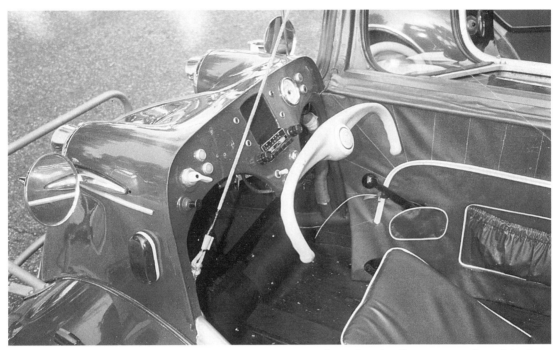

The cockpit of the KR200. The four-speed gearbox was shifted by the lever by the driver's right knee. The handlebar provided quick, three-quarters lock-to-lock turning, leading to somewhat tricky handling. *A. Meyer*

36.25in to 42.5in for greater stability.

Most appreciated was the ability to back up, which was achieved by switching off the engine and then restarting the engine backwards. By pushing the ignition switch in, one activated relays that reversed the windings in the starter so the two-stroke engine was started running backwards. Also, a second set of points was used when the engine was running backwards. The KR-200 also got more conventional pedals for the clutch and throttle in addition to the brake pedal.

Several versions of the KR-200 were sold besides the most common bubble-topped version. First, there was the KR-201 roadster that appeared in 1957. The KR-201 featured a fixed safety glass windshield, side curtains, and a folding fabric top. These items could also be ordered to convert a standard KR-200 to a roadster. The Cabrio-Limousine or KR-200 Kabrio came with framed side windows and a fabric top that could be folded back, replacing the normal domed top.

Finally, there was the "stripped" Sport version which only had a cut-down plexiglass windshield, tonneau cover, and padded cockpit edge strips. It too could be ordered as a conversion kit.

1958-61 Tg 500 "Tiger"

The Tiger was a four-wheeler. The nose section, front suspension, and body-frame were from the earlier models; the remainder of the car was extensively revised. The transverse mounted two-stroke, two-cylinder, 490cc, Sachs engine was rated at 19.5hp, and the four-speed transmission came with a more conventional shift-gate plus a reverse gear.

Besides the Tg 500 coupe that usually featured a lower, "chopped" bubble-top, the four-wheel Messerschmitt came in roadster, Kabrio, and Sport versions, just like the KR-200 series.

When prohibitions on aircraft construction were lifted in 1956, Messerschmitt returned to building aircraft. Fend continued

With Tg 500, the Messerschmitt was becoming more like a regular car, if not in looks, at least in engineering. A more refined swing-axle type rear suspension was now used. *Automuseum Story*

to build cars with a new company called Fahrzeug-und Maschinenbau (FMR) GmbH. In all, about 50,000 Messerschmitts were built before all production ceased in 1964. Of these, about 40,000 were KR-200s and another 10,000 were the earlier KR-175s. Only about 250 Tg-500 models were built.

NSU, NSU-Fiat, and Neckar

NSU, for **N**eckar**su**lmer Fahrradwerke AG, was established in 1873 to build knitting machines, then bicycles and motorcycles.

The 1959-62 Prinz 30 was the final version of the first generation postwar NSU Prinz series. It used the 583cc engine tuned to produce 36hp. *A. Meyer*

Until the late 1950s, NSU was one of the world's foremost motorcycle manufacturers. By 1905, NSU was into automaking, building its own designs and the Belgian Pipe under license. NSU, hit heavily by the depression, had to sell a new factory at Heilbronn. Purchased by Fiat, it produced a variety of Fiat models, including the 500 Topolino under the NSU-Fiat label. One unique model was a two-seat roadster built off the Fiat 500.

After World War II, Deutsche Fiat AG started selling imported Fiats in Germany and by 1950 had resumed production of the Fiat 500C. This was followed by Fiat designs, including the 600. When NSU at Neckarsulm resumed car production in 1958, a dispute arose on the use of the NSU title. This was settled in 1959 with NSU gaining title to the marque, and NSU-Fiat changed its name to Neckar Automobilwerke AG. The latter built several models that were based on Fiats but carried body designs that were often quite different than those built in Italy. These included the Weinsberg two-seat Limousette and Coupe based on the Nuova 500, the Vignale-bodied Jagst 770 Riviera Spyder and coupe, with Fiat 600 mechanics, and the Neckar 850 Adria sedan.

Model	Rating
'58-63 Prinz I/II/III 2-door sedan	★★★
'59-63 Prinz 30 2-door sedan	★★★
'62-73 Prinz 4 2-door sedan	★★★
'64-72 1000 2-door sedan	★★★
'65-72 1000TT/TTS 2-door sedan	★★★★
'59-72 Sport Prinz 2-door coupe	★★★★
'64-67 Wankel Spider convertible	★★★★★
'65-67 110 2-door sedan	★★★
'67-73 1200 2-door sedan	★★★

1958-63 Prinz I/II/III and Prinz 30

The 1958 Prinz, introduced in 1959, was NSU's first car after World War II. The Prinz used a two-cylinder, overhead cam, four-stroke, vertical, air-cooled engine. The 583cc, 26hp engine was mounted in the rear and drove the rear wheels. The four-speed manual transmission was patterned after those used on motorcycles with constant-mesh gears for "easy and silent gear change." A fully independent suspension system used

The NSU Prinz 4 had a definite Chevrolet Corvair look. *Audi*

The 1000TT (Tourist Trophy) featured a 1085cc engine that was rated at 69hp and was fitted with disc brakes up front. The 1000TTS version with a 10.5:1 compression ratio and 85hp was built mainly for racing homologation purposes. *Jim Sykes*

coil springs and wishbones in front and coil springs and swing axles in the rear.

The Prinz had a 78.75in wheelbase and an overall length of only 123.75in. Even so, the Prinz could handle four passengers, and even a fifth in a pinch. This excellent packaging efficiency resulted in some compromises in styling. The unit-bodied car had a very upright greenhouse with excellent visibility in all directions, especially through the large curved glass rear windows. Luggage and the spare tire were carried in the front trunk. The well-constructed Prinz was an immediate hit.

By 1959, there were two Prinz models, the basic Prinz I and Prinz II with deluxe trim and interior fittings. In 1960 through 1963, there were again two Prinz models, the Prinz III with the 26hp, 583cc engine and the 26hp, 583cc engine, and the Prinz 30, which used the same engine but was tuned to produce 36hp. In 1963, NSU produced over 76,000 cars.

1962-73 Prinz 4

The Prinz 4 was a bit longer than the previous Prinz with a wheelbase of 80.3in and an overall length of 135.5in. The engine displacement was increased to 598cc, but horsepower remained at 36. Besides being better looking, the Prinz 4 was roomier inside. The Prinz 4 came in standard and deluxe versions.

1964-72 1000 Series

The NSU 1000 represented a major change for NSU. It now had a four-cylinder, ohc engine. It was still air-cooled and located in the rear. The transversely mounted, 996cc engine produced 51hp. While the styling of the Prinz 4 was carried over, the 1000 was larger with an 88in wheelbase and had an overall length of 150in. With the quad headlights, the 1000 looked even more like the Corvair. There were five versions of the 1000 series starting with the base 1000 and upscale 1000L. The 1000S had further "special" equipment. For ultimate performance, there were the 1000TT and 1000TTS.

1966-73 110 and 1200C

These two NSUs were even larger with a 96.1in wheelbase and an overall length of

While using the Prinz mechanics, including the 36hp twin-cylinder engine used in the Prinz 30, the Sport Prinz's body was designed by Italy's Nuccio Bertone. The coupe's better aerodynamics allowed a top speed of 85mph, about 15mph better than the similarly engined Prinz 30. *Audi*

157.7in. The 110 was powered by the same 1085cc engine as the 1000TT but produced only 66hp. The 1200 used a larger 1177cc version of the air-cooled, four-cylinder powerplant.

In 1969, NSU merged with the Audi NSU Auto Union AG that was owned by Volkswagenwerk. In the next few years, the Audi nameplate would replace NSU. In 1967, NSU had introduced the Ro80 four-door sedan that used a twin-rotor version of the Wankel engine, which had an equivalent displacement of 1000cc. Unlike all previous postwar NSUs, the engine was mounted up front. While a handsome, excellent performing design, there were some reliability problems. The Ro80 was dropped, and the rotary engine technology was sold to Japan's Toyo

The Sport Prinz that rode on a 78.25in wheelbase had an overall length of 141in. While longer than the Prinz sedans, it was really a 2+2 with the rear area suitable for children or a large amount of luggage. *Audi*

The Sport Prinz was the basis of the Wankel Spider which debuted in 1964. This was the first production car to use Felix Wankel's new rotary engine. A single rotor was used in this water-cooled engine with an equivalent of 500cc. Rated at 64hp, the Wankel engine was able to push the Spider convertible to near the 100mph mark. About 2,400 Wankel Spiders were built between 1964 and 1967.

Kogyo for use in their Mazdas. Mazda can be credited with perfecting the Wankel engine. The last NSU, a Ro80, was produced till 1977.

Zundapp

1955-58 Zundapp Janus 250

Zundapp-Werke GmbH switched from munitions to motorcycles after World War I, becoming one of Germany's best known motorcycle brands. Between 1951 and 1985, Zundapp also produced a successful line of motorscooters.

The Zundapp Janus 250 was designed by aircraft-builder Dornier. It had two doors, one at either end of its 114in of overall length. As on the Isetta, they opened like

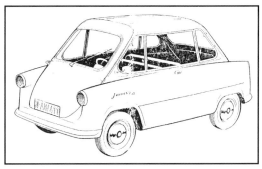

Were it not for the headlights and taillights, it would be difficult to tell which way the Zundapp Janus 250 was going. *Zundapp-Werke GmbH*

refrigerator doors. Four occupants sat on two bench seats, two facing forward and two rearward. The seats folded down to provide sleeping accommodations for two. The name "Janus" was appropriately chosen after the Roman god who faced in two directions.

The motorscooter-based, single-cylinder, two-stroke, air-cooled, 248cc engine was located between the seats and drove the rear wheels. The 14hp engine was able to push the 926lb car to 50mph. Fuel economy was a motorscooter-like 70-plus mpg. The four-speed gearbox used a gate-type hand lever. Other specifications included a 72in wheelbase, 4.40x12 tires, worm-and-nut steering, and hydraulically operated four-wheel drum brakes. The fully independent suspension system used trailing links with coil springs in front and coil-sprung swing axles in the rear. Options included a sun visor for both directions, sunroof, heater, and two-tone paint. About 6,900 Zundapp Janus 250s were built.

'56-58 Janus 250 2-door   ★★★★

Chapter 4

Great Britain

In perhaps no other country has automobile design been as influenced by the tax structure and aimed at dodging, at least partially, high purchase and road taxes. One loophole was three-wheelers. For years, trikes could be licensed as motorcycles with lower taxes, and only motorcycle driver's licenses were needed. Tax advantages also went to buyers who assembled cars themselves. The uniquely British "specialty car" builders

The Austin Seven "Chummy" was the most popular model in the early days. Confusingly, all Seven models were frequently called by this name. This is a 1923 model. *Austin Rover*

mated their chassis and bodies with components from Ford, BMC, Rootes, etc. Most sold their wares in states of completion from turnkey cars to kits in boxes.

Austin

Herbert Austin formed Austin Motor Company, Ltd., in 1905. After several models with mixed success, Austin developed an all-time winner, the Austin Seven.

1922-38 Austin Seven

The Austin Seven succeeded as a "people's car" because, besides being cheap, it was well-engineered and reliable. The design was far from radical, just a scaled-down full-sized car. When introduced, the Seven's four-cylinder, 696cc engine was rated at 10hp. By 1924, it was increased to 747cc and 13hp. Four-wheel mechanical brakes were standard, but until 1931, they were uncoupled in that the foot pedal operated the rear pair and a hand lever for the front brakes. A mechanical starter was available from almost the start, followed by an electric starter in 1923, a major innovation for an inexpensive car. The 800lb car had a top speed of slightly over 50mph and got 40mpg.

The Seven was originally offered as a 2+2 open car, fabric-bodied sedan, and steel-bodied sedan. Through the years, a large variety of vans, delivery vehicles, panel trucks, and pickup trucks were built on the Seven chassis. In the early 1930s, the wheelbase was increased 6in to 81in, the three-speed was replaced by a four-speed, and the gasoline tank was moved to the rear.

When production ceased in 1939, nearly 300,000 Sevens had been produced in England. Versions were built by Rosengart in France, BMW in Germany, Nissan in Japan, and as the American Austin/Bantam in the United States.

Sevens were also clothed with sporty bodies by Austin or outside coachbuilders. Seven-based sports cars started with the 1924 "Sports" with its bobtail rear end and cycle fenders. The Ulster followed in 1928 with a reworked engine coming in normally aspirated or 32hp supercharged forms. The Ulster could hit 75mph with its aluminum

'22-34 "Chummy" touring	★★★★
'26-34 2-door sedans	★★★
'32-35 2-seat roadster	★★★★
'35-38 Ruby roadster	★★★★
'34-38 Ruby 2-door sedan	★★★
'24-37 Sports, Ulster, Nippy, Speedy, Gordon Specials, etc.	★★★★★
'22-37 Vans, panel trucks, pickups, etc.	★★★

body. In 1933, there was the Austin 65 Nippy and the much rarer Austin 75 Speedy. Pioneer aviator E. C. Gordon England not only raced winning Sevens but also built a series of special-bodied sports and race cars around the Seven. These included the Speed Model Seven and the Gordon England Cup Model. Jaguar's parent, Swallow Sidecars, got into the auto business with custom bodies for Austin Sevens.

1953-67 Austin A30, A35, and A40

The all-new Austin A30 was powered by an 803cc, four-cylinder, 30hp engine shared with the 1953-56 Morris Minor. The A30 was the first Austin to use unit-body construction. Other specifications included cam gear steering, independent front suspension achieved via wishbones and coil springs,

While using basically the same mechanics as the original, the mid-1930s Austin Seven received new styling to keep up with the times with features like optional bumpers, trafficators, and "bonnet" vents. This 1936 Austin Seven Opal drophead coupe is owned by Neil Phalen. *Bill Siuru*

The 1953-56 Austin A30 was sometimes called the "Seven" because of its small size (76.5in wheelbase and overall length of 136.4in) and economy of operation. *Barry Sharratt*

'53-56 A30 4-door sedan	★★★
'54-56 A30 2-door sedan	★★★
'54-56 A35 4-door sedan	★★★
'56-59 A35 2-door sedan	★★★
'58-67 A40 2-door sedan	★★
'59-67 A40 Countryman station wagon	★★★

and a rigid rear axle suspended by semi-elliptic leaf springs. Initially, the A30 appeared in four-door sedan form and was joined by a two-door sedan a year later. The A30 had a top speed of 62mph and could deliver 40mpg. The A30 was replaced by the A35, the biggest change being the A-series 948cc, 34hp engine. The extra horsepower increased the top speed to 73mph and fuel economy to a claimed 50mpg.

The 1956-59 Austin A35 used a slightly larger engine in a slightly updated A30 body. *Barry Sharratt*

When Austin modernized its entry-level series, it turned to Pininfarina for a completely restyled body. The A40 series debuted initially as a two-door sedan, joined a year later by the A40 Countryman with a hinged rear window and a drop-down trunk lid. Underneath were the A35 mechanics with little modification. The A-series 948cc engine was used until the 1962 MkII which was fitted with a 1098cc, 48hp engine. The A40's wheelbase was later increased to 83.5in to give rear passengers a bit more room. The overall length was now 144in.

1959-95 BMC Mini

The Mini was designed by Alec Issigonis, who is also credited for the 1948-71 Morris Minor. The Mini pioneered a transverse-mounted engine up front driving the front wheels. The efficiency of the layout is demonstrated by the fact that with an overall length of only 120in, the Mini could accommodate four adults in reasonable comfort plus carry a small amount of luggage in the trunk that opened like a pickup's tailgate.

Unlike most economy-oriented cars, the Mini was fun to drive. The tiny 5.20x10 tires were located essentially at four-corners on a chassis with an 80in wheelbase, which meant minimum overhang. The Mini not only looked like a roller skate, it handled like one.

'59-79 Austin/Morris 2-door sedan	★★
'60-67 Austin/Morris 2-door station wagon	★★★
'60-67 Panel/pickup truck	★★★
'61-66 Riley Elf 2-door sedan	★★★
'61-69 Wolseley Hornet I/II/III 2-door sedan	★★★
'61-64 Mini Cooper (997cc)	★★★★
'64-69 Mini Cooper (998cc)	★★★★
'64 Mini Cooper S (970cc)	★★★★★
'63-64 Mini Cooper S (1071cc)	★★★★
'64-71 Mini Cooper S (1275cc) MkI/II/III	★★★★
'79-95 Mini 1000, 1275 GT, Mini-Cooper	★★
'64-82 Mini Moke (including Australian)	★★★
add one star for convertible conversion	

The Mini's packaging efficiency meant styling compromises, such as a "little two-box" look, body seams, and door hinges on the outside of the car. Through the years, styling was cleaned up a bit by moving the door hinges inside, and wind-up windows in the door replaced sliding ones in about 1970. *Austin Rover*

The basic Mini platform was for a variety of vehicles. The Austin Seven and Morris Mini Minor versions differed only in trim. There were also the Austin Countryman/Morris Traveller woodie station wagon (shown here), a panel van, and pickup. *Bill Siuru*

Upscale Mini buyers could order a Riley Elf (shown here) or the Wolseley Hornet. Between 1961 and 1969, the upscale Wolseley Hornet and Riley Elf featured marque-distinctive grilles, higher trim levels, and "real" trunks. *Bill Siuru*

Mini-Specials

Except for maybe the VW Beetle, no car has been as popular with specialty car and kit builders as the Mini. Many thought they could make the already excellent Mini better, faster, and prettier. On most, you have to look under fiberglass bodies to see the Mini heritage. Builders used any of the Mini's engines, the most desirable being the Cooper-tuned 1000cc and 1275cc units. While born in the 1960s, several are still in production. Here is a sampling.

Minisprint [1965-68]

Chopping and channeling was used to lower the Mini's profile by 3in, removing sheet metal above and below the waistline. After the rake of the windshield and rear window was increased, a new windshield was fitted. Other windows were made of either plexiglass or glass. The front end was redone, with a new steel hood with appropriate fiberglass power budges. Body seams were flush welded, and a fiberglass trunk lid was fitted. About fifty were built. Since 1993, Speedwell Performance Conversions, Ltd., has been replicating the original Minisprint starting with restored Mini Mark I body shells. *Speedwell Performance Conversions, Ltd.*

Mini Marcos (1965-93)

The Mini Marcos was designed by Jem Marsh to use the Mini's front and rear subframes, steering, electrics, suspension, and powertrain. Marcos' contribution was the fiberglass body kit. Through the years, the kits saw several revisions, and of course, many more by the individual builders. An opening hatchback was an option on later Mk III cars and became standard on the Mk IV. The Mk IV, with a floor pan based on the Mini Traveller, allowed a child-sized rear seat or a bit more luggage. In 1976, the car was taken over by D & H Fiberglass Techniques, Ltd., who continued to offer the kit until 1981. The Mini Marcos Mk V, brought back by Jem Marsh after the decade-long hiatus, looked similar to the original, though a few mods were made. Marcos phased out the Mini Marcos in late 1993. Around 1,200 Mini Marcos were built. *Mini Marcos Club*

Midas [1978-95]

Ex-Jaguar engineer Harold Dermott, who ran D & H, completely revised the Marcos design to create the Midas. This fiberglass, 2+2, fastback coupe was more attractive and refined than the Mini Marcos. It was also nearly four times as expensive! By 1983, virtually complete

Midas cars, as well as kits, were offered, and in 1984, there was a turbocharged version. By 1985, there was an improved Midas Gold model that was based on the Austin Metro. D & H was forced into liquidation in 1989. Eventually, the design was picked up by GTM cars, which carried on as Midas Cars, Ltd., and currently offers a nicely styled, Metro-based Midas Gold convertible. *Midas Cars, Ltd.*

Ogle [1962-64]

One of the most attractive Mini conversions was Ogle. The nicely styled, well-finished, and more luxurious two-place GT coupe used BMC Mini parts under a fiberglass body bonded to a strengthened Mini floor pan and cowl. While retaining the Mini's wheelbase and track, the SX 1000 was 12in longer, 2in wider, and 6in lower. An estimated sixty-six SX 1000s were built. *Ogle Design, Ltd.*

In initial form, Minis, including Rileys and Wolseleys, used a four-cylinder, ohv 848cc, 37hp engine, enough to push the 1,300lb Mini to a top speed of around 70mph. Like all Minis, the four-speed transmission was located below the engine in the oil sump. The transverse drive shaft also served as front axles. After 1968, the transmission was fully synchronized. In 1963, a 998cc, 55hp engine became available, first in the Riley and Wolseley, and a year or so later in the Austin and Morris.

The Mini was an unparalleled success in motorsports from the Monte Carlo Rally and the European Touring Car Championship to club racing and parking lot auto crossing. The Mini's excellent handling did not go unnoticed by Formula One car builder, John Cooper. For his first Mini-Cooper, Cooper increased the displacement to 997cc and compression ratio from 8.3:1 to 9.0:1, then added a new manifold, twin SUs, larger valves, and a big-bore exhaust system. Horsepower increased to 55 and top speed to 85mph. The truck-like gear shift was replaced with a more sporting 8in long stick. Seven-inch diameter Lockheed disc brakes replaced the stock drums up front. There were two-tone paint jobs, upscale upholstery, special bumper overriders, and chrome window surrounds. Oil pressure and water temperature gauges were added to the instrument cluster, but no tachometer. There were both Austin and Morris versions.

However, it was the first Cooper S with its 1071cc engine that really transformed the already good Mini-Cooper into a great sports car. This first Cooper S engine had larger intake valves and oil passageways, nitrided camshaft, and strengthened connecting rods for the added output, 70hp. It also used better bearings in the gearbox, a beefed up clutch, 7.5in diameter front disc brakes, and servo-assisted brakes. Top speed was now just over 90mph.

The 1071cc S was replaced by two new versions, the 970cc and 1275cc Cooper S. The two displacements were chosen for their intended racing classes, the Group 2 European Touring Car Championship with a 1ltr upper limit and British and International rallies in

The dune-buggy-like Mini Moke came with a minimum of sheet metal and creature comforts. Initially appearing in 1964, by the end of the decade, it was produced in Australia. *Bill Siuru*

the under 1.3ltr class. These two versions used basically the same engine, the 1275cc achieved by an extra long stroke. The 970cc engine produced 65hp, whereas the 1275cc engine was good for 75hp. The 970cc version was produced only to order and then dropped in 1965. The 1275cc engine was far more amenable to everyday street use.

Through the years of production, 1964 to 1971, the Cooper S came in three versions, the original Mark I, the slightly heavier Mark II in 1967, and the Mark III with roll-up windows in 1970. The lightweight Mark I was the fastest Cooper S with a 100mph top speed.

In all, over 146,000 Mini Coopers were produced, of which about 45,000 were the Cooper S models. This is almost insignificant when compared to the more than five million Minis that have been sold throughout the world, making it by far the best sell-

This Mini-Cooper brochure touts "Hydrolastic Suspension" that was used between 1959 and 1964, but abandoned because of its lack of fore-and-aft pitch control. *Austin Rover*

ing British-built car.

The Mini is still in production as the Rover Mini Cooper 1.3, equipped with a fuel-injected 1275cc engine. The Minis have achieved cult car status in England, Germany, and Japan. The Mini mechanics also got new "clothes" with the Metro that debuted in 1980. The Metro, with updated styling, was a bit longer with an overall length of 134in and an 88.5in wheelbase. The Metros were powered by either the 998cc or 1275cc engine and came as a three- or five-door hatchback. The MG Metro version used the 1275cc engine in normally aspirated or turbocharged form.

Berkeley

Berkeleys were produced by Berkeley Coachwork Company, a house trailer manufacturer. The tiny sports car was designed in 1956 by Lawrence "Laurie" Bond using his experience with light racing cars. Bond is perhaps better known for his three-wheel cars and Bond Equipe coupes. The Berkeleys used alloy-reinforced fiberglass body sections bonded directly to the steel and fiberglass "pont" chassis, a technique developed by Bond. All production Berkeleys used front-wheel drive obtained with a chain drive and a motorcycle-type gearbox. The suspension was independent at all four corners, giving superb handling that was enhanced by a low center of gravity. Up front there were two wishbones with combined springs and shocks. In the rear there were swing

'56-59 322/328cc "Sports"	★★★★
'58-59 492cc "Sports"	★★★★
'58-59 Foursome 4-seat roadster	★★★★
'59-60 B95/QB95 roadster	★★★★
'59-60 B105/QB105 roadster	★★★★
'59-60 T60 3-wheel roadster	★★★
'60 T60 3-wheel coupe/hardtop	★★★
'60 997cc Bandit roadster	★★★★★

axles, again with combined coil springs and shocks. Brakes were drums all around, and Burman worm-and-nut steering was used.

1956-59 Berkeley "Sports" Type SA322 or SE328

The first Berkeleys were fitted with Anzani vertical, twin-cylinder, two-stroke, air-cooled motorcycle engines with a displacement of 322cc and producing 15hp. From early 1957, the Excelsior "Talisman Twin" motorcycle engine was substituted. With a displacement of 328cc, it was rated at 18hp. Both units were mounted transversely well ahead of the front axle. The three-speed motorcycle gearbox had a gate-style gearshift lever. There were neutral positions between gears as well as a main neutral.

While these Berkeleys were fitted with 120mph speedometers, the actual top speed

Of the 4,200 or so Berkeleys built, about 1,700 were three-wheelers. The three-wheel T60 series, which came in roadster and coupe form, was designed for low-cost transportation. The T60 used the 328cc Excelsior "Talisman Twin" engine. *Bill Siuru*

The Berkeley looked quite like the Austin-Healey Sprite, just a bit smaller. Berkeleys were built with either left-hand or right-hand drive. This beautifully restored SE 328 is owned by Tim Klopfenstein. *Gerron Hite*

was only just over half this. The Berkeleys were tiny cars with a wheelbase of only 70in, an overall length of 123in, and 5.20x12 tires. The "328cc Sports" briefly returned in late 1960, fitted with a later SE492 body. Known as a "B65," only about ten were built.

1958-59 Berkeley "Sports" SE492 (500)

This model was powered by a 492cc Excelsior two-stroke, three-cylinder, 30hp engine . The added power allowed the 725lb Sports SE492 (500) to reach 75mph and still turn in 50-plus mpg. A "Foursome" was also available with a longer 78in wheelbase and overall length of 131in to carry four people, albeit not in great comfort. Berkeley roadster buyers could opt for a detachable fiberglass hardtop along with side curtains with sliding glass windows. These cars differed from the earlier SE322 and SE328 by having a more vertical leading edge to the doors, a slightly different windshield, and a four-speed gearbox.

1959-60 B95/QB95 and B105/QB105

While still motorcycle-based, these cars used four-stroke engines with overhead valves and two cylinders. The 692cc Royal Enfield "Super Meteor" 40hp engine was used in the B95/QB95 version, and the Royal Enfield "Constellation" offered 50hp for the B105/QB105. The numbers in the designations represented the factory's claims for the model's top speed. In reality, the top speeds were about 10mph on the optimistic side. The rare "QB" versions were a bit longer with a 78in wheelbase and an overall length of 133.5in. The "B" versions used the older short body and chassis. The added length on the QBs mainly went into increased trunk space. The B95 and B105 also had a nose job that included a somewhat higher hoodline and a squarish grille, compared to the earlier sleeker front end design.

The Berkeley's days were numbered with the advent of the Austin-Healey Sprite. The Sprites were more car for less money. Berkeley tried to compete with its Ford-powered Berkeley Bandit, but it was too expensive. Only a couple of prototypes were built. The marque folded in 1961, but the company continued to build trailers.

Bond

While built by Sharps Commercials Ltd., the name came from Laurie Bond who did the designing. In 1965, the company became Bond Cars, Ltd. By 1969, the marque had been absorbed by Britain's most successful three-wheel manufacturer, Reliant.

Early Bond Minicars came without doors, just cutaways, but later models got doors. A fabric top and side curtains provided protection from the elements. *Register of Unusual Microcars*

While initial Bonds were two-seaters, by 1954 four-seat versions were added. About the same time, Bonds got a more "real" car look with front fenders, though, of course, they were not needed to cover wheels. *Register of Unusual Microcars*

'48-53 Minicar	★★★
'51-55 Sharp Minitruck	★★★
'53-58 Minicar Mk B/C/D	★★★
'58-61 Minicar Mk E/F	★★★
'59-65 Ranger van	★★★
'61-65 Minicar 250cc	★★★
'65-70 Bond 875cc	★★★
'70-74 Bond Bug	★★★★

1948-65 Minicar

The first Bond Minicar was powered by a single-cylinder, two-stroke, air-cooled, 122cc Villiers motorcycle engine that drove the single front wheel via a roller chain drive. Soon, a 197cc, 8.5 or 9hp Villiers engine was substituted. The design included a three-speed, motorcycle-type transmission shifted via a dashboard-mounted lever but without a reverse gear. Reverse was added in 1957. By 1952, an electric starter, combined with the generator, replaced the previous underhood kickstarter. Top speed was 45mph and up to 85 to 100mpg was possible.

Bonds used unit-body construction with the first ones, featuring a stressed skin aluminum body. Later cars used a combination of aluminum, steel, and fiberglass. The front suspension used a trailing arm with a coil spring over the shock absorber. Until 1953, only the tires absorbed road shocks in the rear, then an independent rear suspension with trailing arms and rubber-torsion springing was added. The worm-and-sector steering for the single front wheel swiveled through almost 180deg, the reason why reverse was thought unnecessary. This gave a turning circle of only 9ft from a car with a 65in wheelbase and overall lengths varying between 104 and 120in. Brakes were mechanical, and a front brake was added in 1953.

Between 1951 and 1955, a three-wheel Sharp Minitruck delivery van joined the passenger car offerings. By 1958, there was a 246cc Villiers reversible engine and a four-speed transmission.

1965-74 Bond 875 and Bond Bug

Bond had dropped the Minicar line in an attempt to satisfy the needs of more sophisticated consumers. The replacement was the

The Bond Bug's two-passengers rode in an air-craft-style cockpit that was hinged at the front for entry. While there was a roof, side curtains with plastic windows were still used. *Ogle Design, Ltd.*

Bond 875, the designation coming from the 875cc, four-cylinder, Hillman Imp engine that now mounted in the rear and drove the rear wheels. The car also used other components from the Imp, including the four-speed, all-synchronized gearbox and trailing arm independent rear suspension system. A commercial Bond 875 van was also offered.

The final Bond was the Bond Bug, which was touted as a three-wheel sports car. While labeled a Bond, the futuristic three-wheeler was developed by Reliant and used Reliant's 700cc, later 750cc, four-cylinder engine in the rear. Bond Bugs, painted orange, were frequently photographed with three wedged into a single parking space.

The Fairthorpe Atom was a rather crude, basic transportation car.

Fairthorpe
1955-60 Atom and Atomota

Fairthorpe, Ltd., was founded in 1954 by Air Vice-Marshal D.C.T. Bennett of World War II RAF fame. The Atom series came with a variety of BSA air-cooled, motorcycle engines mounted in the rear and driving the rear wheels using a three-speed gearbox.

The Atoms, available from 1955 through 1956, used a backbone chassis and a fiberglass body that kept the weight to under 900lb. They had an 89in wheelbase, 132in overall length, and a fully independent suspension system using swing axles and coil springs on both axles.

The follow-on Atomota featured a restyled fastback coupe body characterized by fenders that extended far beyond the deck. Exposed door hinges were just one example of the crudeness of the Atomota's plastic body. While smaller with an 81in wheelbase and a 129in overall length, the Atomota was a 2+2 coupe. Power came from a two-cylinder, air-cooled, 646cc, 35hp BSA motorcycle engine. A four-speed transmission was used. The front suspension came from the Standard Ten, and there was a live axle in the rear.

1955-74 Electron and Electron Minor

The Fairthorpe Electron was a more conventional, front-engine, rear-drive, sports car. The Austin-Healey Sprite-sized roadster featured a fiberglass body mounted on a simple tubular-ladder frame. Fairthorpe sold cars in both kit and completed form. Most Electrons used the potent 1098cc, Coventry-Climax engine that produced 71, 84, or 93hp. The Electron was one of the smallest (82in wheelbase and 144in long), lightest (995 to 1,150lb), and cheapest cars to use the Coventry-Climax engine. Top speed was an impressive 110 to 120mph.

By 1956, there was the first of the less expensive and somewhat smaller Fairthorpe

'55-57 Atom Mk I/II/IIA/III coupe	★★★
'55-57 Atom Mk I/II/IIA/III convertible	★★★★
'58-60 Atomota coupe	★★★
'55-63 Electron MkI/II/III	★★★★★
'56-63 Electron Minor	★★★★
'63-74 EMS Mk III/IV/V/VI	★★★★
'61 Electrina 2-door sedan	★★★★

Electron Minors, or EMs (81in wheelbase and 120in overall length). The Electron Minor Mk I used the 948cc, four-cylinder, 38hp engine from the Standard Ten, plus many of its other mechanics, including the wishbone and coil-spring suspension system and four-speed transmission, modified for sports car duty. Top speed of these less potent Electrons was about 90 to 95mph. The Electrons and Electron Minors had a 2+1 seating arrangement where the +1 sat rather uncomfortably between the regular two occupants.

The 1960 Mk II used a twin-carbureted version of Triumph Herald's 948cc engine, plus its running gear. Front disc brakes were optional. The 1963 Mk III was about 8in longer but used the same chassis and suspension. Power usually came from the 1147cc Triumph Spitfire engine, but some Mk IIIs were fitted with a 997cc four-cylinder from the Ford Anglia. The Mk III was the first Fairthorpe to come with a hardtop as standard equipment, though a soft top was available.

The 1967 Mk V used a further lengthened body that allowed 2+2 seating. The bulge in the hood was for the 1296cc Triumph Spitfire engine. Disc brakes were fitted on all four wheels. The 1972 EM VI had a slightly restyled body. The Triumph-based independent suspension system was retained as was the Spitfire engine. It is estimated that about 750 Mk I through Mk VI Electron Minors were built.

Model	Type	Displ	Hp	Top Speed
Mk I	ohv, 1-cylinder	249cc	11hp	45mph
Mk II	ohv, 1-cylinder	248cc	17hp	55mph
Mk IIA	rotary valve 2-cylinder, 2-stroke	322cc	15hp	55mph
Mk III	ohv, 2-cylinder	646cc	35hp	80mph

The Anglia (shown here) and Prefect were the first "captive" imports when Ford attempted to market them in the United States. Here, the larger 1172cc engine was used, and the Brits could order the same combination as the Anglia Ten. American buyers were not quite ready, and at $1,000, they were no competition for full-sized Fords that were only $200 to $400 more. *Ford of England*

Both the Anglia and Prefect (shown here) carried over prewar styling and mechanics. Stylewise, the two were quite different, and the Prefect was a bit more modern, but not much. *Ford of England*

The Anglia (shown here) and Prefect that appeared in 1954 bore a strong resemblance to the slab-sided 1949-51 American Fords, only smaller.
Ford of England

Ford of England

The first Ford was sold in England in 1903 and after 1911, Model Ts were assembled there. The 1932 Model Y was the first Ford designed for the European market. It used a 933cc, side-valve, four-cylinder engine. Like the other British Fords, the Model Y looked like a scaled-down version of American Fords, not surprising since much of the designing was done in Dearborn.

The Model Y was replaced by the New Eight or Model 7Y in 1937, which evolved into the Anglia by 1939. By 1935, Ford was also offering a slightly larger Model C with a 1172cc, side-valve, four-cylinder engine which evolved into Prefect in 1938.

'46-53 Anglia 2-door sedan	★★★
'46-53 Prefect 4-door sedan	★★★
'54-59 Popular 2-door sedan	★★★
'54-59 Anglia 2-door sedan	★★
'59-62 Popular 2-door sedan	★★
'54-61 Prefect 4-door sedan	★★
'56-61 Escort/Squire station wagons	★★
'60-67 Anglia 2-door sedan	★★
'62-64 Anglia Estate 2-door station wagon	★★★

1946-53 Anglia and Prefect (also 1954-59 Popular)

Anglia and Prefect production resumed immediately after the war with essentially prewar models. This meant mechanics that dated back to the 1932 Model Y and 1935 Model C. These included antiquated features such as a front I-beam axle and a rigid rear axle, transverse leaf springs, worm-and-nut steering, and mechanical brakes.

The two-door Anglia rode on a 90in wheelbase while the four-door Prefect had a 94in wheelbase. The Anglia used the 933cc engine, whereas the Prefect had the 1172cc engine. Both were mated to a floor-shifted three-speed.

When the new Anglia and Prefect came out in 1954, Ford "simplified" the old two-door Anglia, calling it the Popular, and cut the price for the home market. It had the 1172cc engine, three-speed, and mechanical brakes.

1954-61 Anglia, Prefect, Escort, and Squire

Ford of England's smallest cars were completely redesigned for 1954. The two-door was still the Anglia, and the Prefect

In 1956, two two-door station wagons were added. The base Escort used the Anglia front end and grille, whereas the upscale Squire (shown here) followed the Prefect's styling and featured wood bodyside trim and a bit more chrome. The mechanics were identical. *Ford of England*

was the four-door; however, both now used the same 87in wheelbase. There were variations in trim and different grilles. These new Fords used unit bodies and a modern independent front suspension that included MacPherson struts. Semi-elliptic leaf springs were used in the rear.

While having a completely new body, the Anglia and Prefect retained the old 1172cc engine, but power was boosted to 36hp, and other improvements were made. A floor-shifted, three-speed gearbox was still used. After the Anglia received a completely new body in 1960, the four-door Prefect and station wagons soldiered on through 1961. The Prefect did get the Anglia's new ohv, 997cid engine and four-speed transmission. However, the Escort and Squire wagons continued to use the old 1172cc engine and three-speed transmission. The old style Anglia with the 1172cc engine also continued for a few more years as a replacement for the previously budget-oriented Popular.

1960-67 Anglia and Anglia Estate

The two-door Anglia was restyled for the 1960 model year. Also new was a 997cc, ohv engine. Although smaller than the 1172cc engine it replaced, there was an increase in horsepower to 41. For the first time in any British Ford product, there was a

The post-1960 Anglias featured a "Z" reverse slanting rear window patterned after those used on Mercurys and Lincolns, but it did not open. The reverse slant allowed greater rear seat headroom and a larger trunk lid opening. *Ford of England*

Besides the Anglia two-door sedan, there was also a two-door Estate Car and a small panel van. *Ford of England*

The Frisky's body styling is credited to Italy's Michelotti and included a curved windshield. *Register of Unusual Microcars*

four-speed transmission. By 1964, the Anglia could be ordered as a "Super" that featured a 1198cc, 53.5hp, four-cylinder shared with the Ford Cortina. All Anglias shipped to the United States after 1965 came as the Anglia 1200, meaning the 1198cc engine.

Frisky

The Frisky minicar was designed by Captain Raymond Flower for production in Egypt. The 1956 Suez crisis intervened, and production never commenced. Henry Meadows, Ltd., a well-known British engine and gearbox manufacturer, picked up the design.

1957-61 Frisky Sport and Coupe

The initial Frisky was a four-wheeler with closely spaced rear wheels eliminating the need for a differential. The front thread was 48in while the rear was only 32in. Unlike the steel prototype, the production cars had a fiberglass body mounted on a separate, twin-tube, welded-steel chassis. Two body styles were offered, the two-passenger Frisky Sport roadster and the Frisky coupe, which could carry two adults and a couple of children. Both had a 60in wheelbase and an overall length of 109in. The hardtop coupe, which was identical to the roadster

'57-61 Frisky Sport	★★★★
'57-61 Frisky coupe	★★★★
'58-59 Prince	★★★
'61-64 Family Three	★★★

above the waistline, had sliding side windows while the roadster had side curtains.

Power came from a rear-mounted, two-stroke, 325cc, 16hp air-cooled Villiers (or sometimes an Excelsior motorcycle engine) that drove the rear wheels via a chain drive. The Sports version got two more horsepower via a higher compression ratio. The four-speed, motorcycle-type, constant-mesh gearbox was shifted by a selector on the right-hand wheel well housing that protruded into the cockpit. There was no reverse gear. To back up, one shut the engine off and then restarted the engine running backwards. A combined generator/starter, in which the current flow in the windings could be reversed, was used.

Other specifications included a Dubonnet-type independent front suspension while in the rear there were motorcycle-type hydraulic shock absorbers integrated with coil springs for the live rear axle. Hydraulic drum brakes were fitted to all four wheels (some early models had only three drum brakes), and cam gear steering was used. A 60 to 65mph top speed and 60mpg were claimed.

1958-64 Family Three and Prince

Guy, who produced the Frisky's fiberglass bodies, took over the company from Meadows. The name was changed from Meadows to Frisky Cars, Ltd. Frisky began offering three-wheel models with a 197cc single-cylinder Villiers or, after late 1959, a

The Frisky Family Three was basically a Frisky coupe with one less wheel and a smaller engine. It could accommodate two adults and two small children. *Register of Unusual Microcars*

Kaz Wysocki's 1959 Frisky Prince. Few Princes were built before production of Friskys of all types ceased in 1964. Reportedly, only two exist today. *Kazmier Wysocki*

248cc twin-cylinder Excelsior engine. The ads touted a 50mph top speed, 75mpg, and a mere five pound British tax. The Prince was a somewhat larger, two-door, three-wheel, two-seat coupe. Power came from a 325cc Villiers or Excelsior engine. Between 500 and 1,000 Friskies were built, of which about 300 were three-wheel Family Threes.

Hillman (Including Sunbeam and Singer)

Rootes Motors, Ltd., controlled several well-known British marques, including Humber, Hillman, Singer, and Sunbeam. None offered a real minicar until the Imp. Rootes not only developed the revolutionary new Imp, but also built completely new manufacturing facilities near Glasgow, making the Imp the first car produced in Scotland since the 1920s. The Imp's development proved very costly, to the point that Rootes needed outside financial help from Chrysler. By 1967, Chrysler had total control of Rootes and changed the name to Chrysler UK, Ltd., in 1970.

'63-76 Hillman Imp 2-door sedan	★★★
'67-76 Imp Californian/Stilleto/	
Chamois 2-door coupe	★★★★
'65-76 Husky 2-door station	
wagon and Commer van	★★★
add one star for Super Imp, Imp Sport,	
Sunbeam Sport, and Singer Chamois	

1963-76 Hillman Imp (and derivatives)

The Hillman Imp was Rootes' attempt to compete against the best-selling Austin/ Morris Minis. While the Minis used a trend-setting transversely mounted front engine and front-wheel drive, the Hillman used a rear engine, never popular in British cars and, by the 1960s, a bit obsolete. However, these cars were fast and handled well. On the street, they were very good; on the track, they were fantastic.

The 875cc, four-cylinder, sohc, all-aluminum engine was based on a Coventry-Climax design and was canted 45deg for a lower center of gravity. Depending on year,

The Hillman Imp was the Rootes Group's answer to the hot-selling BMC Minis. *Bob Allan, Imp Club*

Imp-based Specials

Ginetta G15 [1968-1974]

The G15 was Ginetta's best known model with over 800 made. Done right, G15s did not have a kit car look. Underneath there was a channel-section steel chassis bonded to the lower half of the fiberglass body and floor pan. The 875cc engine produced 55hp in stock form and had the radiator up front for improved cooling. A common upgrade was the 998cc version of the Imp engine, producing 65hp, and in the hands of tuners, over 120hp. While most of the running gear was pure Imp, the front suspension came from the Triumph Herald/Spitfire. The Ginetta G15 got Triumph 9in disc brakes. Touted as a "Luxury Sports Coupe—100mph/ 40mpg," it offered creature comforts such as a heater, collapsable steering column, and leather/aluminum steering wheel. *Roger Bryson*

Clan [1971-74]

The Clan Motor Company, Ltd., was founded by Paul Haussauer, who left Lotus in early 1970 taking several other Lotus employ-

ees with him. The styling of the Clan Crusader's fiberglass body was done by John Frayling of Lotus Elite, Elan, and Europa fame. Again, the 875cc Imp engine was used, but the radiator remained in the rear. The engines used in the Clan, like in the G15, had larger inlet valves, a hotter camshaft, twin 1.25in Stromberg carburetors, and a free-flow, four-branch exhaust system. The Clans retained the Imp's front swing axle suspension and 8in drum brakes. Only 315 Clan Crusaders were built. A majority of the Clans were factory built, but some were sold in component form. *Chris Clay*

Davrian [1967-83]

In 1965, Adrian Evans built a plywood-bodied prototype roadster around the Imp floor pan and mechanics. Production cars used a fiberglass body. Davrian Developments, Ltd., was founded in 1967. Davrians were sold as kit or as almost finished, rolling chassis. There were both road and competition versions. Mk I and some Mk II cars were open top models. The rest through the Mk VIII were two-seat coupes.

model, and market, horsepower ranged from 37 to 52. The fully independent suspension system used coil springs surrounding telescopic shocks and swing axles in front. The independent rear suspension used coil springs and semi-trailing links on detachable subframes. The four-speed transmission was fully synchronized. Drum brakes and rack and pinion steering were used. The unit body Imp rode on an 82in wheelbase and had an overall length of 145in, over 2ft longer than the Minis. The Imp used "normal" 5.50x12 tires compared to the Mini's 10in ones, a point mentioned in the Imp brochures.

Initially, the Imp came as a two-door,

While there were many modifications in body design and styling through the years, the body and chassis consisted of a monocoque center section with three major basic moldings. Other pieces included doors and separate bolt-on front and rear sections with removable access panels that allowed easy styling updates. There were many different front-end configurations—round or rectangular headlights recessed into the fenders, "pop-up" headlights, and completely faired-in front ends with or without headlamps on the pure competition cars. Those that wanted more power could opt for the 998cc version of the Imp engine, turbocharging, or even 1040cc and 1200cc versions. The Imp's front swing axle and rear semitrailing suspension were used, but special lightweight Davrian versions were available as options on the Mk VIII. While early models used the Imp's drums, Davrian developed a four-wheel disc brake system for the Mk VIII that could be adapted to all Imps. From the Mk IV, slide-down windows replaced sliding ones, and some earlier cars were sometimes retrofitted. *John Rawlins*

The Sunbeam Stilleto coupe was a bit prettier than the basic Imp sedan. There was also a corresponding Hillman Californian and Singer Chamois coupe version. *Bob Allan, Imp Club*

"almost" hatchback. Only the rear window opened, and the liftover was quite high because of the rear engine. A fold-down rear seat augmented the smallish front trunk where some of the space was taken by the spare tire. There were many variants. Imps sold in the United States were marketed as Sunbeams. In England and other countries, there was an upscale two-door sedan called the Singer Chamois that was added in 1964, followed by an upgraded Imp Mk 2 and Super Imp with a new cylinder head and larger carburetor. The Imp Sport appearing in late 1966 included a 52hp engine and power brakes. Sunbeam and Singer got corresponding models. In 1967, two more models were added, a two-door coupe, called the Hillman Californian Imp, and a Husky station wagon. Badge-engineered versions of the coupe were also sold as the Sunbeam Stilleto and Singer Chamois coupe. The final addition was the luxurious and pricey 1975 Hillman Caledonian. The Imp and its variants were dropped in 1976 after a total of about 440,000 had been built over a thirteen-year period.

Lloyd

Lloyd Cars Ltd., was established by Roland Lloyd, a proponent of the two-stroke engine that, while very popular on the Continent, was seldom used in British cars.

1936-39 Lloyd 350

The original Lloyd was a simple, ultra-light roadster. Power came from a 347cc, two-stroke, single-cylinder, water-cooled engine. The rear-mounted engine drove only one of the rear wheels via a three-speed

LLOYD "350" TWO-SEATER.

The 1936-39 Lloyd 350 had its one-cylinder, 347cc engine in the rear. While water-cooled using a thermosyphon system, the radiator was mounted in the rear. The radiator grille was just for looks. *John Lloyd*

'36-39 350 2-door roadster	★★★★
'39 350 Van	★★★
'48-50 650 2-door roadster	★★★★

transmission and chain drive. There was a backbone chassis and an independent suspension system all around that used transverse leaf springs. The 350 had a 69in wheel-

While the 1948-50 Lloyd looked like a decent sports car, it offered poopless performance with its 654cc, 17.5hp, two-stroke, two-cylinder engine. Weighing in at 1,344lb without people, it took over a half minute to accelerate to 40mph, and top speed was a mere 46mph. *John Lloyd*

base and an overall length of only 111in.

The car sold initially for a very low British seventy-five pounds. In 1939, Lloyd began offering an equally simple van costing only fifteen pounds more. Some 250 cars and vans were built up through 1939.

1948-50 Lloyd 650

The postwar Lloyd that appeared in 1946 in prototype form was a more ambitious vehicle with quite attractive styling. The 650 was larger than the 350, with a 93in wheelbase and a 147in overall length. Only one body style was offered, a 2+2 roadster. While saloon and van prototypes were built, neither reached production.

Power came from Lloyd's own 654cc, vertical twin, two-stroke engine that produced a mere 17.5hp. The engine was mounted transversely at the front of the tubular backbone chassis and drove the front wheels. The four-wheel independent suspension system used horizontal coil springs in front and vertical coil springs in the rear. The coil springs were housed in oil-tight cylinders, eliminating the need for conventional hydraulic shock absorbers. Brakes were still mechanical, and the transmission had three speeds. Production ceased in 1950 with some 350 to 400 built.

Morris

William Morris (later Lord Nuffield), who first marketed bicycles and motorcycles, offered his first car, the Morris Oxford, in

The Morris Minor 1000 station wagon turned out be a pretty handsome vehicle. Styling remained pretty constant through the nearly quarter century of Minor production. A simpler, rectangular grille with horizontal bars appeared in 1955, and by 1956, a single, curved windshield replaced the previously used two-piece, flat-glass one. *Bill Siuru*

'48-71 2-door sedan	★★★
'48-71 2-door convertible	★★★★★
'51-71 4-door sedan	★★★
'54-71 2-door station wagon	★★★★
'53-71 Pickup/panel	★★★★

1913. The first under-1ltr Morris was the 1928-34 Minor with an 847cc four-cylinder engine. This Minor, designed to compete against the highly successful Austin Seven, did not sell that well. Its greatest claim to fame is the first 1928 M-type MG Midget, which was created off the Morris Minor. The Minor was replaced in 1934 by the far more successful Morris Eight with a 918cc, four-cylinder

The Minor was the first British model to go over a million units, which occurred in 1961. When production of the Minor ceased in 1971, more than 1.3 million units had been built. *BMC*

Morris offered a pickup built using the same Morris Minor passenger car components. *Bill Siuru*

Reliant is still producing the three-wheel Robin three-door hatchback (shown here) and the Rialto, which comes as either a station wagon or a commercial van. Reliant is the last company to be seriously marketing three-wheelers. They still use a fiberglass body on a galvanized steel frame. *Reliant Motor, Ltd.*

engine. The Eight was returned to production after World War II until its replacement, the all-new Morris Minor, was ready.

1948-71 Morris Minor

The Morris Minor, designed by Alec Issigonis, was Britain's answer to the Renault 4CV, Citroen 2CV, Fiat 500, and Volkswagen. However, with its water-cooled, four-cylinder engine up front driving the rear wheels, the Minor was a far more conventional car. Initially, the unit-body-constructed car came as a two-door sedan and convertible, where the window frames remained in place.

The Minor's wishbone and torsion bar front suspension was quite advanced for its day. In the rear there were long semi-elliptic leaf springs and a solid rear axle. Shock absorbers were of the lever type, and rack and pinion steering was used. Other specifications included hydraulic drum brakes and a four-speed gearbox. This was all packaged within an overall length of 148in and an 86in wheelbase, with a weight of around 1,700lb.

The Minor was powered by a succession of engines. Initially, the prewar 918.6cc, L-head, 27.5hp unit was used. After the Nuffield Organization and Austin merged in 1952, the Austin A30's 803cc, overhead valve, four-cylinder engine rated at 30hp was used in the Minor. In 1957, a 37hp,

948cc engine shared with the Austin A35 was used. Now it was called the Minor 1000. The final upgrade came in 1963 with the substitution of a 1098cc, ohv engine that was rated at 48hp, but the model was still the Minor 1000. Both 1000 versions had a top speed near 75mph, about 10mph more than the cars with the 918.6cc and 803cc engines.

Reliant

In 1935, Tom L. Williams founded Reliant Engineering Company, Ltd., to build three-wheel vans. Williams had designed the Safety Seven three-wheeler while employed by Raleigh Cycle Company, Ltd. He acquired the design rights to the three-wheel van after Raleigh abandoned car and truck production. Up until 1952, Reliant concentrated on three-wheel vans with JAP motorcycle engines. In 1938, motorcycle engines were replaced by the 747cc, four-cylinder Austin Seven engine. Initially, the engines were purchased from Austin, but after Austin dropped the Seven, Reliant built the engine until 1962 under license from Austin.

1952-95 Reliant Regal, Robin, and Rialto

Reliant's first car was the three-wheel, slab-sided Regal four-passenger roadster followed shortly by a four-passenger coupe. The under-900lb Regal could be registered as a motorcycle, and only a motorcycle license was needed. The 1952-55 Regals used sheet metal panels attached to composite hardwood framing mounted on a pressed rail frame. The Regals had a 74in wheelbase and an overall length of 123in.

The Regals were powered by the 747.5cc, 16hp, four-cylinder engine which was located between the front seats and drove the rear wheels via a four-speed gearbox. The spare tire and tools were stored under the hinged hood lid, and there was cargo space in the rear.

The suspension used a torsion bar with a double-acting shock absorber. The rear suspension consisted of semi-elliptic leaf springs with double-acting shock absorbers. Hydraulic drum brakes were used on all three wheels. The factory claimed a 65mph

'52-61 Regal (Mk I-VI) three-wheel roadster	★★★★
'56-61 Regal (Mk I-VI) three-wheel coupe	★★★★
'62-67 Regal 3/25 three-wheel sedan	★★★
'64-74 Rebel four-wheel sedan	★★★
'68-73 Regal 3/30 three-wheel sedan	★★★
'73-95 Robin three-wheel sedan	★★★
'75-84 Kitten four-wheel hatchback	★★★
'82-95 Rialto three-wheel Estate	★★★

top speed and 45 to 60mpg.

Through the years, the Regal was improved several times. For instance, the 1956 Mk III version had a one-piece fiberglass-over-ash frame body. The 1961 Mk VI got a bit more interior room via an extended roofline.

The Regal was replaced in 1962 by the Regal 3/25. The designation refers to the three wheels and the 25hp produced by the new Reliant engine. The four-cylinder, ohv, 598cc engine is considered to be Britain's first all-aluminum engine. Through the years, the engine was enlarged—700cc in 1967, 750cc in 1972, and 848cc in 1975. Other changes on the 3/25 included a new unitary body of bonded inner and outer fiberglass moldings on a steel chassis.

1964-74 Rebel and 1975-84 Kitten

Reliant launched the Rebel, a small four-wheeled sedan. The four-passenger Rebel also used a fiberglass body mounted on a steel chassis. Power came from the 598cc engine. As with the three-wheelers, the Rebel's engine grew in displacement. The Reliant Rebel was superseded by the four-wheel Kitten in 1975. The Kitten was offered in sedan, station wagon, and van versions. The Kitten used the 848cc engine.

1958-65 Scootacar

Unique even among the unique British micro cars were the three-wheel Scootacars offered by Scootacars, Ltd. The original prototype was built by a British locomotive manufacturer as a shopping car for his wife.

More Than a Motorcycle, Less Than a Car

Favorable taxing and licensing policies, plus low transportation costs, led to a rather long menu of three-wheelers for British buyers. Besides Berkeleys, Bonds, Friskies, Reliants, Scootacars, and Trojans, there were several other lesser British known three-wheel minicars. Several German microcars of the 1950s and 1960s, namely the Isetta, Messerschmitt, and Heinkel/Trojan, were sold in Britain in three-wheel form. Here are a few more.

The Gordon (1956-58) was a rather simple, open-bodied, two-seat, three-wheeler. While looking a bit like the contemporary Bond and Reliant, its single-cylinder, two-stroke, 197cc Villiers engine was mounted outside of the vehicle on the right side next to the driver. The engine drove only one wheel via a chain. At the time, it was the cheapest car on the British market.

The Powerdrive (1956-58) was a three-wheel roadster with an aluminum body. The rather wide car could seat three abreast. Power

came from a 322cc, two-cylinder, two-stroke Anzani engine mounted transversely behind the seat driving the rear wheel via a chain.

A common misconception is that the Coronet (1957-60) was basically the same design as the Powerdrive. This is not the case. While also designed by David Gottlieb and having a similar three-wheel layout, the Powerdrive and Coronet were quite different cars. For starters, the Powerdrive had an aluminum body while the Coronet's was made from fiberglass. Beneath, there was a different chassis. The Powerdrive used Austin suspension and steering components, whereas the Coronets came from the Standard Eight. The Coronet used an Excelsior 328cc twin with 18hp. Top speed was just under 60mph, but nearly 60mpg was possible. Perhaps 250 to 500 Coronets were built. *Register of Unusual Microcars*

The three-wheel Peels [1962-65] were among the smallest cars ever built. The original P50 single-seater with an overall length of only 53in was not much more than a seat in a box with windows. Power came from an equally tiny 49cc, 4.2hp, single-cylinder, two-stroke DKW engine in the rear driving the single rear wheel. The "upscale" Trident was a bit larger and able to seat two, barely. Almost the entire body was hinged at the front, so it could be opened for entry. The top consisted of a perspex bubble canopy without windows. Openings in the sides of the body and a small front vent brought in some fresh air. Again, the 49cc DKW engine was used. There was a three-speed transmission, but reverse consisted of a handle on the rear of the body. The interior was equally spartan with a single-spoke steering wheel whose column's universal joint was from a 1/2in drive socket set. There was not even a speedome-

It turned out so well he decided to put it into production. Between 900 and 1,000 of these tiny cars were built.

'58-63 Mk I	★★★★
'60-65 Mk II	★★★★
'61-65 Mk III	★★★★

1958-65 Scootacar Mk I, Mk II, and Mk III

The Scootacars were tiny, with a 54in wheelbase, an 87 to 95in overall length, including the rear-mounted spare tire, and a width of only 52in. Scootacar was really more scooter than car. Steering was done via

ter, but then top speed was only 30mph. About seventy-five Tridents were built. *Register of Unusual Microcars*

a scooter-like handlebar, and the driver and passenger straddled a true "bench" seat equipped only with small seatbacks in the Mk I version. Later versions had a bucket seat for the driver and an obliquely positioned bench seat behind for the passenger.

Scootacars weighed between 500 and 630lb, depending on the "Mk." The Mk I and II were powered by a Villiers 197cc two-stroke, single-cylinder, 8.4hp engine under the bench seat which drove the rear wheel. Mk IIIs used a 324cc Villiers, twin-cylinder, 16.5hp, two-stroke engine. The Mk III, also called the "Deluxe Twin," was a bit longer, 95 versus 87in. The body was also a bit more curvaceous with the rear-mounted spare tire coming as standard equipment.

The Scootacars were advertised as being capable of carrying two adults and a child to a top speed of 49 to 68mph. Fuel consumption was a rather impressive 55 to 58mpg.

Standard and Triumph

R. W. Maudslay founded the Standard Motor Car Company, Ltd., in 1903. Standard's rather extensive line-up included a succession of cars with relatively small-displacement, four-cylinder engines. These included the 1913 Rhyl 9.5 (1087cc), 1928 Nine (1155cc), and 1932 Little Nine (1006cc).

The Triumph nameplate evolved from bicycles in 1887, to motorcycles in 1902, a three-wheel car in 1903, and the first four-wheel car in 1923, the Triumph 10/20. Triumph's first really successful model was the 1928 Super Seven with a 747cc, four-cylinder engine, which was soon enlarged to 832cc. Designed as a direct competitor to the Austin Seven, it featured hydraulic brakes versus the mechanical ones on the baby Austin.

In 1945, Standard acquired Triumph, which had been in receivership since just before the war broke out. During the war, the Triumph factory in Coventry was destroyed by German bombing raids. In 1961, Standard-Triumph became part of the British Leyland empire. The last Standard car was produced in 1963, and the Triumph nameplate lasted until 1984.

1939-48 Flying Eight

The Standard Flying Eight was the first small British car with an independent front suspension system. Power came from a 1009/1021cc, L-head, four-cylinder engine, nominally rated at 28hp. Several models were available on an 83in wheelbase, including two- and four-door saloons, a "touring"

model with 83,139 built when production ceased in 1948.

1953-61 Eight, Ten, Companion, and Pennant

The Standard Eight unit-body, four-door sedans rode on an 84in wheelbase and were powered by an 803cc, ohv, four-cylinder engine. They featured coil spring independent front suspension and a live rear end. To keep costs down, the very basic model lacked a rear trunk opening, had sliding windows in the front doors, and like the Triumph TR2, lacked a front grille cover.

The Scootacar has four speeds forward and backward! Reverse was engaged by shutting the engine off and restarting it by depressing the key to have the engine run in the reverse direction. *Bill Siuru*

drophead coupe, and a roadster. Styling was typically 1930s with a rather stubby profile, separately mounted headlamps, and a flowing vertical grille. It was a very popular

The Scootacar was a "high-profile" vehicle with its narrow width and height that provided headroom for the tallest driver. It had a fiberglass body

placed over a steel chassis and a door only on one side. *Bill Siuru*

Standard Ten station wagons being assembled. The Ten was sold on the American market as the Triumph TR10 to capitalize on the TR2/3's good image. *Triumph*

Standard-Triumph had Giovanni Michelotti design the rather angular Triumph Herald. *Triumph*

In 1954, the Eight was joined by a somewhat less spartan Ten saloon, with a trunk lid, and the Ten Companion four-door station wagon. Engine displacement was increased to 948cc which produced 40hp. Options on the Tens included a two-pedal semiautomatic transmission. A more luxurious model named the Penchant appeared in 1957. Some 310,000 of all types had been made.

1959-71 Herald (All Versions)

While called a Triumph, the Herald was really a replacement for the Standard Eight and Ten. The Herald came initially in either "fixed-head coupe" or "drophead coupe" forms. Until 1961, the Heralds were powered by a somewhat anemic 948cc, four-cylinder, ohv engine that had previously been used in the Standard Ten. Depending on the market, the 948cc engine produced 40 to 45hp, and with twin SU carburetors, 50hp. This was matched to a four-speed transmission that was synchronized on the upper three gears. The independent front wishbone and coil spring suspension also came from the Standard Eight/Ten while the all-new independent rear suspension used swing axles, transverse leaf springs, and radius rods. Drum brakes were standard, but disc front brakes could be ordered as an option on later models. The car rode on a 91.5in wheelbase, and it was 153in long.

Things were improved a bit in 1961 when a 1147cc, 43hp engine was used in the Herald 1200, and after 1967, a 1296cc, 70hp four-cylinder in the 13/60 series. The Triumph 1200s sold in the United States had the 1147cc engine uprated to 51hp. By using a separate body on a backbone chassis, it was rather easy to add new versions like a two-door saloon and Courier Van in 1961 and a two-door station wagon in 1967. The complete hood folded forward for excellent access to the engine and suspension system. A muscle car of sorts was created when the Triumph 1998cc, six-cylinder engine was placed in the Herald body to create the 1966-71 Vitesse. This had been preceded by a somewhat tamer Vitesse 1600 from 1962 to 1966 that used a 1596cc, six-cylinder engine.

'39-48 Flying Eight 2/4-door sedan	★★★
'39-48 Flying Eight roadster	★★★★★
'39-48 Flying Eight tourer	★★★★★
'53-59 Eight 4-door sedan	★★
'54-59 Ten 4-door sedan	★★
'54-61 Ten Companion estate	★★
'57-59 Pennant 4-door sedan	★★
'59-71 Herald convertible	★★★★
'59-66 Herald 2-door coupe	★★★
'63-67 Herald 2-door sedan	★★★
'67-71 Herald 2-door station wagon	★★★
'61-67 Courier van	★★★

Fred Lieb bought this Turner Sports 950 in 1959 and has raced it ever since. Compared to the initial 850, the mildly restyled body included fins topping the rear fenders. *Gordon Jolley*

Beau Gabel's Turner Mk I at speed. *Gordon Jolley*

Turner

John (Jack) Turner, a grassroots racer with a talent for building race cars and engines, founded Turner Sports Car, Ltd. Series-produced Turners starting in 1955 were comparable in size, amenities, and performance to basic British sports cars like the Austin-Healey Sprite and MG Midget. Turners garnered many trophies, including winning four *Autosport* Championships overall in 1958 and 1959 and for under 1300cc cars in 1961 and 1962. A large percentage of the Turners were exported to the United States, where they did well in SCCA competition, mainly because of their light weight and excellent handling. Turners came in either completed or kit form.

'55-56 803 roadster	★★★
'56-59 950 roadster	★★★★
'59-60 Sports Mk I roadster	★★★★
'60-63 Sports Mk II roadster	★★★★
'63-66 Sports Mk III roadster	★★★★
'62-64 GT coupe	★★★★★

add one star for cars with Coventry-Climax engines

1955-56 Turner 803

The 803 used the 803cc, four-cylinder engine from the Austin A30 as well as its four-speed gearbox. In stock form with a single Zenith carburetor, it produced 30hp. The two-seat, tubular-braced fiberglass body was bonded to the ladder frame chassis with the main tubes joined by crossmembers front and rear, the basic design that would be used throughout the Turner's life. Up front the pressed steel wishbone and coil spring suspension was taken pretty much intact from the A30. The rear suspension was designed by Turner and incorporated transverse laminated torsion bars with twin trailing arms, a solid rear axle, tubular shocks, and a Panhard rod. Weighing in at around 1,200lb, the 803 was able to do an honest 80mph. The 803 had an 80.5in wheelbase and was 138in long and 54in wide. This was a basic sports car with spartan accommodations, a minimum of creature comforts, and suicide doors. Depending on the source, between 75 and 100 Turner 803s were built.

1956-59 Turner 950

The Turner 950 used the 948cc, Austin A35 engine in the 803 chassis. The engine came in two states of tune. With a single Zenith carburetor, it put out 34hp, and with a single SU, 40hp. With the latter, top speed was around 90mph. A second series in 1958 got twin SU carburetors and 43hp. About 150 Turner 950s were reportedly built.

1959-60 Turner Sports Mk I

The Turner received a major redesign with the Turner 950 Sports Mk I. It had a much sleeker and wider-appearing body. The doors were now conventionally hinged, the tailfins were gone, and the grille was squatter and wider. Power usually came from a 60hp, 948cc, twin-SU-carbureted engine. About 150 Mk Is were built.

1960-63 Turner Sport Mk II

The Mk II Sports had a less spartan interior and better instrumentation. Even so, Turners would never be known for their fit and finish. Most used Ford powerplants, initially in 997cc, 1098cc, or 1340cc form. With the Ford engines, one got a coil spring and wishbone front suspension borrowed from the Triumph Herald. In 1963, the Mk II Sport got a large airscoop. By 1963, a twin-carbureted Ford 1499cc engine with a modified head and twin SU carburetors producing 80hp was very often specified.

1962-64 Turner GT

The Turner GT was the rarest of all Turners with only nine produced. The GT was a 2+2 coupe and most refined of all Turners. Besides the entirely new body, there was a revised chassis that resembled a box-section arrangement with a steel floor pan welded on. The front suspension came from Triumph, and coil springs, trailing arms, Panhard rods, and telescopic shocks were found on the rear. Disc brakes and wire wheels were standard. Most, if not all, GTs were fitted with the 1500cc Ford engine which gave a 110mph top speed.

1963-66 Turner Mk III

The final Turner was the Turner Sports GT Mk III with facelifting that included a revised hood and rear. The car was equipped with the Ford 1499cc engine. Wire wheels became standard. In the past, they had been optional, although most buyers had opted for them.

Alexander Turners and Turner-Climaxes

Alexander Engineering, a Turner distributor, made some modifications of its own, namely fitting Mark Is and IIs with disc brakes, close-ratio gearboxes, and an Austin-Healey Sprite engine with their own cross-flow cylinder heads. The Alexander-modified cars were real screamers, able to top 100mph.

Starting with the 950-series, Turner customers could opt for the more potent Coventry-Climax overhead camshaft, four-cylinder engines. Included was the 1097cc Coventry-Climax FWA engine rated at 75hp. Even more potent was the 1216cc Climax FWE, which was also found in the Lotus Super 95 Elite, and depending on the state of tune, produced between 75 and 105hp. The Climax-powered cars, often called Turner-Climaxes, could run circles around cars like the Austin Healey Sprite and had a top speed of 100-plus mph.

Chapter 5

Italy

The Italian automobile industry can be summarized by a single word, Fiat. In some years, 90 percent of the new cars sold in Italy were Fiats. Besides being the largest Italian auto maker, the Fiat's parts bins have been used to produce other marques such as Abarth, Autobianchi, and Moretti. Fiat has acquired several Italian makes—Autobianchi

The Tipo 508 Balilla was one of Fiat's early small cars with 124,165 produced between 1932 and 1937. While its basic 995cc engine produced 22hp, a version used in the 508S two-seat Spider was good for 36hp, and famed tuner Gordini got 50hp out of the engine. *Fiat*

in 1968, Lancia in 1969, Abarth in 1971, Alfa-Romeo in 1987, and a 50 percent share of Ferrari in 1969. With Fiat's virtual dominance, Italian consumers who wanted a domestically produced minicar have been pretty much limited to Fiats or Fiat-based cars. Those who wanted a bit different styling could opt, for example, for an Autobianchi, or for higher performance, a Fiat Abarth.

Because of Italy's lower economic conditions compared to most of industrial Europe, low-cost and high-mpg minicars with quite small displacement engines have been popular. Low wages plus high vehicle and gasoline taxes kept Italians out of the car market much longer than their neighbors to the north. Even in the late 1950s, there was only one car for every fifty Italians.

Fiat's monopoly of the Italian auto market also brought obligations to the "state," and sometimes Fiat's decisions were politically driven. For instance, political pressure to provide a very low-cost vehicle, especially for much poorer southern Italy, reportedly influenced Fiat to produce the tiny Nuova 500. When the initial price of the 500 came in

near that of the larger Fiat 600, the "social" price was dropped and a 25,000 lire rebate was returned to those who had already bought cars.

Fiat

The Fiat empire all began in 1899 when Emanuele di Bricherasio, Giovanni Agnelli, and Count Roberto Biscsaretti di Ruffia formed *Fabbrica Italiana Automobili Torino*, or Fiat. With the first Fiat, the Tipo A, using its 697cc, rear-mounted, flat twin, Fiat started out by building small cars but soon moved upscale. Up until the early 1920s, Fiat produced a large number of different models in relatively small quantities, concentrating on

'36-48 500A Berlina/ Trasformabile	★★★★★
'48-49 500B Berlina/ Trasformabile	★★★★★
'49-54 500C Berlina/ Trasformabile	★★★★★
'48-55 500B/C Belvedere	★★★★★
'37-54 500A/500B/500C Furgoncino	★★★★★

The Fiat 500 Topolino as it appeared when introduced in 1936. The spare tire fit into the rear of the rear deck, bumpers were not fitted, and door windows were of the sliding type. *Fiat*

Fiat Around the World

Fiat products have been built in many other countries starting in 1912 when they were built in Vienna by Austro-Fiat. Since then, others have been produced in Argentina, Brazil, Chile, Columbia, Czechoslovakia, England, Egypt, India, Ireland, Indonesia, Malaysia, Morocco, New Zealand, Portugal, Thailand, Venezuela, Zambia, and a few more countries. Simca started out by building Fiats, and NSU built them for many years. Fiats produced by Crevena Zastava in Yugoslavia are better known as Yugos, and the former U.S.S.R. got extensive assistance for its Volzhsky Avtomobilny Zavod (VAZ), sold as Ladas. Fiats were even built in Poughkeepsie, New York, in 1910.

One of Fiat's most successful ventures was *Sociedad Espanola Automoviles de Turismo* (SEAT), a joint venture between Fiat, the state-owned Nacional de Industria, and six Spanish banks. Models included the SEAT 600/600D and 850, coming not only as two-door sedans as in Italy but also as a longer-wheelbase, four-door sedan that was not built in Italy. By the end of the 1960s, SEAT was

The SEAT 600 went into production in 1957 and remained in production until 1973, three years longer than in Italy. *SEAT*

the luxury and middle-class cars. Fiat's first small car produced in large quantities was the Tipo 509 (1925-29) with a 990cc engine.

1936-55 500 Topolino

The Fiat Topolino, affectionately called the "Mickey Mouse" or "Little Mouse," was Fiat's first minicar. The Fiat Tipo 500 that

Spain's largest auto maker. The SEAT 127 went into production in 1973, and there was a four-door version that was even exported to Italy. Even after VW displaced Fiat in 1980, SEATs still were Fiat-based, like the SEAT Marabella that was technically similar to the Fiat Panda, or the SEAT Ibiza available with a Fiat-designed 903cc engine.

Austria's Steyr-Daimler-Puch built Fiat-based cars between 1949 and 1978. The Steyr-Puch 500, introduced in 1957, was the Nuova 500 with slightly altered styling but with a Steyr air-cooled, opposed-twin, 493cc engine which grew to 643cc. There also were more sporty 650T and 650TR versions. A station wagon was virtually the same as the Autobianchi-built Giardiniera. Steyr's next car was based on the rear-engined Fiat 126 but with the Steyr 643cc air-cooled twin.

These were not the first Steyr mini-cars. In 1936, Steyr-Daimler-Puch AG introduced the Type 50. This was a unit-body, two-door, fastback sedan powered by an opposed 984cc, four-cylinder engine. For the 1938 Type 55, the engine grew to 1158cc and 25hp. Some 13,000 Type 50s and 55s were built before production ceased in 1940.

The SEAT 850 was produced from 1966 until 1974 while it was dropped from production in Turin after 1971. *SEAT*

first appeared in 1936 was powered by a four-cylinder, side-valve, water-cooled engine with a displacement of 569cc and 13hp. The radiator for the thermosyphoning cooling system was located behind the engine to give added passenger space on a wheelbase that was only 79in long. The car was only 121in long, and weighed about 1,300lb. For a

The Topolino was significantly modernized with the 500C, which was a couple of inches longer, had bumpers that were part of the body, and headlights integrated into the fenders. *Fiat*

The Belvedere station wagon was offered in both 500B and 500C shown here) versions. *Fiat*

The *Furgoncino*, from 1936, was a rather nice-looking panel truck. This is a 500C version. *Fiat*

The Fiat 600 Multipla was more minivan than station wagon. In many parts of the world, it was used as a taxi. *Merkel Weiss*

very low-cost car, the Topolino had such features as four-wheel hydraulic brakes, four-speed transmission, and independent front suspension using a transverse semi-elliptic spring. In the rear there was a live axle suspended by quarter-elliptic springs, which were changed to semi-elliptic springs in mid-1938. Worm-and-sector steering was used, and tires were 4x15s. The Fiat 500 came as a Berlina two-door, two-passenger coupe, and a *Trasformabile*, a Berlina with a fabric sunroof.

The original design was produced until 1948 when the 500B appeared to replace the 500A, though the "A" was not an official designation. Besides minor cosmetic changes, the engine got an ohv cylinder head and a 6.5:1 compression ratio to increase the horsepower to 16.5. Other changes included telescopic shocks and a

rear sway bar. The basic design was given a major facelift for the 500C. With a top speed of 55mph and being capable of getting 50mpg, the Topolino was perfect for the cash- and fuel-poor Italian economy. When the last 500C Belvedere rolled off the production line in 1955, 519,646 Topolinos had been produced.

1955-70 Fiat 600 and 600D

The Fiat 600 was Fiat's answer to the Renault 4CV and Volkswagen Beetle. Like these two, the 600 had a rear-mounted engine, four-wheel independent suspension, unit-body construction, and could carry four. Of these three, the 600 had the smallest engine, a mere 633cc that produced 28.5hp.

The 1960 Fiat 600D got a bigger engine (767 versus 633cc), and suicide doors were gone by 1964. *Fiat*

Michael Antonich's beautiful Fiat 600 Jolly is a concours winner. The cut-down doors made for easy entrance and exit but precluded the use of any type of side curtain. *Michael Antonich*

'55-60 600 Berlina	★★★
'60-70 600D Berlina	★★★
'56-60 600 Multipla	★★★
'57-61 600 Jolly	★★★★★

The four-cylinder, water-cooled engine had a 7.5:1 compression ratio, three main bearings, ohv, cast-iron block, aluminum cylinder head, and a single carburetor. The four-speed, floor-shifted transmission and differential were installed as a unit with the engine, and the rear wheels were suspended by swing axles. The 600D had a displacement increase to 767cc and 32hp. Top speed was only about 60mph, and it took fifty-four seconds to get there. Initially, the 600 came

Abarth

Carlo Abarth and CSrl developed about 200 different models. While many were race cars or "one-off" prototypes, several were mass produced. A good-sized book, such as Peter Vack's *Illustrated Abarth Buyer's Guide*, is needed to cover all the Abarth models. The Fiat 600 was not only the fodder for a vast number of Abarths, but the car that made Abarth a full-fledged auto maker.

Abarth first offered aftermarket performance parts and complete "Derivazione" kits for the 600. Soon Abarth was building complete cars around the 600. Abarth's TC (Turisimo Competizione) series not only used

This Fiat Abarth 850 TC features an auxiliary radiator up front and the propped up rear engine lid that helped cure the Abarth's chronic cooling problems. *Merkel Weiss*

the Fiat 600's mechanics but also the two-door sedan body, albeit with improvements and modifications. Each successive TC model was a more radical departure from the original Fiat 600.

The initial Fiat Abarth 750 Berlina used the 600 engine bored and stroked to 747cc and tuned for 40hp (47hp in the Mille Miglia). Body changes were limited to Abarth's own "grille" with Scorpion logo, hood ornament, and "Derivazione 750" markings. By the final 1000 TC Radiale, there were more significant styling changes. A radiator enclosed in a fiberglass housing was grafted on up front. Auxiliary front-mounted radiators were first used on some of the 850 TC Nurburgrings. At the rear, a permanent fiberglass whale tail (first used on the 1000 Corsa) replaced the propped-up engine lid that had been characteristic since 1959.

"Radiale" signified the hemispherical combustion chambers in an entirely new head that was still bolted to the basic 600-based block. The Radiale engine made 108hp, and by 1970, 112hp. Throughout the life of the TC series, significant changes were also made to the Fiat 600's fully independent suspension system to enhance handling. The 1000 Corsa was capable of 115mph, almost twice that of the basic Fiat 600. There were improvements in braking with front disc brakes first used on the 850 Berlina Series I and four-wheel disc brakes available on the 1000 Corsa.

Year	Model	Displacement	Horsepower
'56-59	750 Series Berlina	747cc	40-47
'60-65	850 Berlina Series I	847cc	52-55
'62-64	850 TC Nurburgring	847cc	60, 68
'62-64	1000 TC	982cc	60-66
'64-68	1000 Corsa	982cc	76, 80, 85
'66-70	1000 TC Radiale	982cc	108, 112

in two-door sedan form, with 600s fitted with fabric sunroofs being called convertibles. There was luggage space behind the rear seat and in a small compartment up front. By 1958, the rear seat folded down for more cargo capacity.

The four-door Multipla station wagon appeared in 1956. While built on the 600 chassis and using mostly 600 mechanics, the Multipla was somewhat larger. While using the same 78.75in wheelbase as the 600 Berlina, its overall length of 141in was 10in longer. It was also 7in taller.

The convertible edition was the same vehicle with a fabric sunroof. The four- or five-seat Multipla was considered a "sleeper type" station wagon; whereas the other version sat six passengers.

Fiat offered the 600s mainly for basic, economical transportation. However, it called on Ghia of Torino to convert 600s into the Jolly. The Jollys first appeared in 1957 using 600 mechanics and sheet metal. They were completely topless with a temporary "surrey" top providing protection only against the sun and a sudden summer shower. Besides their limited utility, they were significantly more expensive than the regular 600 sedans. When production ceased in 1970, Fiat had built over 2,604,103 Fiat 600s.

1957-75 Fiat Nuova 500

The Fiat Nuova 500 debuted in the summer of 1957 as a replacement for the Topoli-

This nicely restored Nuova 500 Jolly belongs to Hubert Onstad. Note the "surrey-with-the-fringe-on-top-look" and the "tacked-on" headlights needed to meet US requirements. *H. H. Onstad*

no. This microcar with an easily obtained 55mpg fuel economy appeared at just the right time; the Suez Crisis of 1956 had sent a fear of oil scarcity throughout Europe.

'57-73 Nuova 500 Berlina	★★★
'57-64 Nuova 500 Jolly	★★★★

The tiny car was a mere 116in long and had a 72.4in wheelbase. Power came from a 479cc, two-cylinder, rear-mounted engine. The upright, in-line, four-stroke engine was

This Fiat Nuova 500 has the "tacked-on" headlights required on cars sold in the United States. Normally, bumpers were fitted. *Bill Siuru*

This Nuova 500 Jolly is a European model, as noted by the integrated headlamps. *Courtesy Janet Westcott, GB Fiat 500 Club*

Moretti

When Giovanni Moretti founded Fabbrica Automobili Moretti SpA in 1945, he had already been building motorcycles for two decades, and his SANEM three-wheel trucks were popular during World War II.

Moretti produced a large number of different models, none produced in substantial numbers. La Citas minicars were built between 1945 and 1948 and were powered by Moretti's own front-mounted, vertical, twin-cylinder, 350cc, 14hp engine. Sedan, coupe, and station wagon versions were offered.

In the 1950s, Moretti built most all the components including engines in-house. In the mid-1950s, the Moretti catalog included coupes, spiders, four-door sedans, "Competizione" sports racers, and even cab-over-engine station wagons. Between 1952 and 1961, Moretti also offered small trucks and taxis. Engines included 592cc, 747cc, and 1204cc four-cylinder powerplants both in single cam and twin camshaft form. Also listed were 820cc and 980cc single-cam engines. Moretti's low production proliferation of models and inhouse-built componentry added up to quite expensive cars that were essentially hand assembled, though body parts were sometimes interchangeable between models.

The 1950-58 Moretti 600 series consisted of Berlina coupes, convertibles, and station wagons built on an 82in wheelbase, These front-engine, rear-drive cars were powered by Moretti's 592cc, single-overhead camshaft, water-cooled, four-cylinder engine. Most cars had aluminum bodies on a steel tubular backbone chassis.

There were even more models in the 1954-60 Moretti 750 series. The initial Berlina

The Moretti 750 series was its most popular series. This is a 1959 Moretti 750 coupe. *Bill Siuru*

The tiny 1967-69 Sportiva coupes used the floor pan from the Fiat 850 sedan as well as its 50hp engine and other mechanics. Optional powerplants included a more potent 850 spider engine and a 1000cc engine with 62hp. *Merkel Weiss*

air-cooled. A four-speed transaxle was fitted but was nonsynchromesh to cut costs. When introduced, the engine was rated at 13hp, but by the fall of 1957, power was upped to 15hp in the Standard Nuova 500, which also featured better interior trim and windows. The 500 came with a folding fabric roof, fixed rear quarter windows, and vent panes in the front door windows. While early 500s did not have roll-down door glass, later ones did. Suicide doors were retained until the 1965 500F. By 1958, the horsepower was 16.5hp.

There were several changes for 1959. First, there was a Sports model with a two-cylinder 499cc engine, and the compression ratio was increased from 7:1 to 8.6:1 to obtain 21hp. The Sport version could hit 66mph, 10mph more than the standard model. There were also new models such as a Nuova convertible which was really just a sedan with a

coupe and Barchetta roadster were joined in about 1958 by a spider convertible, GT coupe, four-door sedan, and station wagon, the latter featuring a cab-over-engine design so up to seven could be carried. The Moretti 750 Gran Sport Berlinetta was a particularly desirable model, as were the Tour du Monde coupes and spider. These Morettis were sometimes called "baby Ferraris" because of the fine styling and engine sounds.

By the 1960s, Moretti had abandoned much of its independence and was building special-bodied, Fiat-based cars and light trucks. Moretti-bodied, Fiat-based models ranged from a two-seat coupe based on the Nuova 500 all the way up to a very expensive spider based on the Fiat 2300 with the six-cylinder engine increased to 2.5ltr. In between, Fiat 600Ds, 850s, 1300s, 1500s, 124s, 125s, 128s, and so forth were treated to the Moretti touch and sold under the Moretti label. Typically, these were upscale berlinettas, sedans, coupes, and spiders. There were several commercials based on the rear-engine Fiat 600D platform.

In more recent years, the Moretti label has been used on several sport utility vehicles using Fiat mechanics. For instance, in the early 1970s there was the Midimax that looked much like the contemporary Citroen Mehari. The Midimax was based on the front-wheel-drive Fiat 127. Other "fun" cars of the 1980s included the open-top Moretti Uno Folk, the 4x4 Moretti Panda Rock, and the Moretti Uno Country, a multipurpose vehicle based on the Fiat Uno.

Merkel Weiss' beautiful 850 Spider with later-model headlights and aftermarket front air dam. The Spider's smooth lines were spoiled a bit after early 1968 when the front end was revised and the "frog-eye" headlights replaced the previously covered ones. *Merkel Weiss*

1964-73 850 Sedan, Coupe, and Spider

The Fiat 850 sedan replaced the 600. While the four-passenger 850 sedan provided entry-level transportation, the sports cars built off the 850 platform were more exciting. The styling of the 850 Spider and 2+2 fastback Coupe was very different—the Spider was designed by Bertone whereas the Coupe was done by Fiat designers. Fiat added an additional model in 1970 done by Bertone, the 850 Sport Racer, with a vinyl-covered hardtop permanently bolted atop the Spider body.

'64-71 850 2-door sedan	★★
'65-73 850 Spider	★★★★★
'65-71 850 Coupe	★★★★
'65-71 850 Racer	★★★★

Regardless of the body style, they all used the same four-wheel independent suspension system with a transverse-mounted leaf spring, triangulated upper control arms, an antisway bar, and double-acting shock absorbers in front. In the rear there were semitrailing arms, coil springs, an antisway bar, and double-acting shock absorbers. The 850 sedan, Spider, and Coupe had a 79.8in wheelbase. Unlike the base 850 sedan with four-wheel drum brakes, the Spider and Coupe had disc brakes up front.

The sports car, four-cylinder, water-

fabric sunroof that now rolled all the way back. Ghia also produced a 500 Jolly. Like the 600 version, the top was cut off, then some new sheet metal was added and seams were smoothed with lead and body filler. The job was finished with a cutdown windshield, surrey top, and basket weave seats. Some 3,612,928 Fiat 500s had been produced when production ceased in 1975.

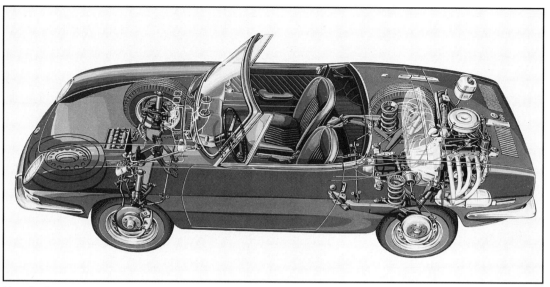

Nuccio Bertone assigned famed stylist Giorgio Giugiaro the task of designing the 850 Spider.

Underneath the mechanics were from the Fiat 850 sedan. *Fiat*

cooled, 843cc engine used until 1968 put out 52hp, about 25 percent more than in the 850 sedan. This was done mainly by increasing the compression ratio and using a two-barrel carburetor. From 1968 to 1969, 850s imported into the United States used a slightly smaller 817cc engine to get around emission requirements that then applied to engines with displacements over 50cid or 820cc. After 1969, displacement was increased to 903cc with horsepower upped to 58hp. All 850s had a fully synchronized, four-speed transmission. Instrumentation on the Coupe and Spider included a tachometer, mostly

The same mechanics were used in the 850 Coupe, but the body designed by Fiat's own de-

sign team, headed by Mario Boano, was completely different. *Fiat*

With an overall length of 142in, the Coupe was billed as a four-passenger car; it was really a 2+2. The Spider, though 6in longer, was strictly a two-seater. After 1968, Coupes got quad headlights. *Fiat*

gauges rather than idiot lights, and a rather optimistic 100mph speedometer (120mph in the Racer). The Coupe had a top speed of around 85mph, and the Spider was good for about 5mph more.

While the Coupe and Racer were dropped after 1971, the Spider soldiered on until 1973 when it was replaced by the X1/9. The 850 was Fiat's only rear-engined sports car. Counting all models, Fiat built 2,203,380 cars in the 850 series.

1970-94 126, 127, Panda, and Uno

The Fiat 127 was Fiat's best-selling model until 1982. Actually, the car first appeared in 1969 as the Autobianchi A112. The 127 could be ordered with the 903cc, front-mounted, four-cylinder engine as well as 1049cc and 1301cc engines produced in Brazil. A 1301cc, four-cylinder, diesel engine became available in 1981. Other features included a four- or five-speed transmission, front disc brakes, and a limited slip rear differential. It came in either three- or five-door hatchback form.

The very modern, front-wheel-drive Panda became Fiat's smallest car in 1980. Pandas were three-door hatchbacks. *Fiat*

The front-wheel-drive Uno that debuted in 1983 came as three- and five-door hatchbacks. *Fiat*

'72-81 126 2-door sedan	★★
'70-83 127 3/5-door hatchback	★★
'80-94 Panda 3-door hatchback	★
'83-94 Uno 3/5-door	★

The Fiat 126, developed from the Nuova 500, would be Fiat's final rear engine car. Initially, its two-cylinder, air-cooled engine had a displacement of 594cc, which was increased to 650cc. Equipped with a four-speed transmission, the 126 could carry four passengers to speeds up to 65mph.

In 1980, Fiat's smallest car became the Panda with an overall length of 134in. Initially, 652cc, 843cc, and 903cc four-cylinder engines were used. Later engine options included 770cc, 999cc, and 1108cc engines. A 4x4 Panda used a 968cc and then a 999cc engine.

The somewhat larger front-wheel-drive Fiat Uno was available with the 903cc, 1049cc, and 1301cc engines from the previous 127 series. There was also a 1300cc diesel engine that came from Fiat Automoveis in Brazil. Later engines included 999cc, 1392cc, 1499cc, and 1301cc four-cylinder engines; the 1301cc was turbocharged. Horsepower ratings were from 44 to 100hp for the Uno Turbo.

The Fiat 500 Bianchina was a 500 fitted with a more sporty coupe body. It was a two seater with space behind the seats for small children or luggage. The front trunk was pretty much filled by the spare tire and gasoline tank. *Bill Siuru.*

Autobianchi

Eduardo Bianchi was not only Italy's premier bicycle and motorcycle maker but also an important producer of cars and commercial vehicles for more than four decades. While production of trucks, motorcycles, and bicycles resumed after World War II, auto making did not start again until 1957, and then under a newly formed Autobianchi SpA, which involved Fiat, Bianchi, and Pirelli. By 1963, the company was wholly owned by Fiat, and by 1968, "Sezione Autobianchi" became part of Fiat SpA.

'57-68 Bianchina 2-door coupe	★★★★
'60-67 Giardinera station wagon	★★★★
'60-67 Bianchina convertible	★★★★★
'60-67 Bianchina 2-door sedan	★★★★
'69-86 A112 2-door hatchback	★★★
'71-84 Abarth A112 Berlina	★★★★

1957-69 Bianchina and Giardinera

The tiny Bianchina coupe was built off of the Nuova 500 platform. The Bianchinas had a unitized, all-steel body. Power came from the same 479cc, two-cylinder, rear-mounted engine. By 1960, the more powerful 499cc engine was fitted.

The Giardinera four-passenger station wagon was also built off the Nuova 500. The two-cylinder engine was mounted horizontally to increase the cargo capacity. Other Bianchina models included a rare convertible and an upscale two-door, four-passenger sedan achieved by basically extending the coupe's roof and using a near-vertical rear window.

1969-86 Autobianchi, Lancia, and Abarth A112

Sezione Autobianchi often tested the market for new Fiat models. One of these was the A112, which paved the way for the Fiat 127. The A112 was a two-door sedan with front-wheel drive and a transversely mounted four-cylinder, water-cooled engine. Initially, the A112s used the 903cc Fiat engine, but running in the opposite direction and producing 44hp. Subsequently, a 968cc engine was used

In 1971, Abarth began building a tuned

version of the 903cc engine. By 1973, the displacement on the Abarth A112 was increased to 1049cc, and output was 70hp for a 100mph top speed. A five-speed transmission was available after 1978. Abarth completely modified the engines before delivering them to Autobianchi for installation. The Abarth A112s also got slight fender flares, mag-style wheels, Abarth badges, and an upgraded interior, including a leather-covered steering wheel, sport trim, and an enhanced instrument package.

The A112s, including the Abarth versions, were marketed by Lancia. The A112 was an extremely successful car with about 1.2 million built by 1985. The A112's replacement was the Y10, a modern econobox using a variety of four-cylinder engines with displacements from 999cc to 1301cc, including turbocharged versions. A four-wheel-drive version was offered from 1986. The Y10 was built by Autobianchi but sold either as an Autobianchi Y10 or Lancia Y10.

Innocenti
1961-65 Innocenti A40
Innocenti Societa Generale per l'Industrie Metallurgia e Meccancia began auto making when it obtained a license to assemble CKD (complete knock-down kits) Austin A40s in Italy. Innocenti was best know for its Lambretta motorscooters.

Styled by Pininfarina, the station wagon-like, two-door, A40 sedan already had an Italian heritage, though the mechanics were pure Austin. The Innocenti A40 initially used the 948cc four-cylinder engine, but by 1963, the larger 1098cc engine was available.

'61-65 Innocenti A40 2-door sedan	★★★
'61-70 Innocenti spider and coupe	★★★★★
'65-72 Mini 2-door sedan	★★★
'65-74 Traveller/T1000 2-door station wagon	★★★★
'72-74 Mini 1000/MiniMatic/1001	★★★
'72-74 Mini-Cooper 1300 2-door sedan	★★★★
'74-82 Innocenti (Bertone) Mini 1000/1300	★★★

In 1963, Innocenti began production of the IM3, a somewhat modified BMC Morris 1100 four-door. In 1965, there was the J4, an Italianized Austin 1100. While engines and other componentry came from Britain, bodies were built by Innocenti.

1961-70 Spider and Coupe
Innocenti offered its own version of the Austin-Healey Sprite. The Innocenti 950 sports car used Sprite mechanics, but the 948cc engine did eventually have twin carburetors for a bit more power, up to 56hp. Designed by Ghia, virtually all body panels were different, and it was a very pretty car. Innocentis had roll-up windows long before the English counterparts did. The rare coupe version had no British counterpart. By 1965, the Innocenti S roadster was using the 1098cc, 59hp engine, and by 1968, the 1275cc, 65hp engine.

1965-74 Innocenti Mini
Innocenti's most successful models were those based on the BMC Mini. The Innocenti Minis had better trim than their British cousins and were sold to Italians who wanted a better handling and more fashionable alternative to a Fiat.

Production of the Innocenti Mini started with the two-door sedan, and an Italian version of the Mini Traveller was added in 1967. By 1972, the Innocenti Mini line-up had grown to include the 998cc Innocenti Mini 1000, a Mini Matic, the Mini T1000 estate, deluxe Mini 1001, and the Mini-Cooper 1300 with the 1275cc engine.

In 1972, Innocenti was taken over by British Leyland, and there was a restyled "new" Mini done by Bertone. A modernized and attractive Innocenti Mini, now a hatchback, debuted in late 1974. The completely new body still used the Mini floor pan and other mechanics, thus retaining the Mini's character and handling. The new Innocenti Mini 1000 still used the 998cc engine while the 1275cc engine powered the Mini 1300 version.

In 1975, BL, in financial trouble, closed the Innocenti operation, and it was handed over to the Italian government. By 1976, the

The 1937-49 Lancia Ardea used a 903cc, four-cylinder engine in a body highly influenced by the trend-setting Lancia Aprilia. Like the Aprilia, this was a pillarless, four-door sedan with unit body construction. *Lancia*

company was back in operation. De Tomaso turned it back into a profitable operation. The company was renamed Nuova Innocenti SpA, and the Bertone-styled Minis were sold as the Innocenti Mini de Tomaso. In 1981, Innocenti began switching over to Daihatsu three-cylinder engines. Initially, a 993cc engine was fitted into the Bertone-style Mini body, which was renamed the Innocenti Tre. By 1983, a diesel version of the 993cc engine was also offered, as well as the Turbo de Tomaso, which featured a turbocharged, 72hp version of the same engine.

By the late 1980s, the models were designated the 990, 990 Matic, and the Mini-diesel/990 diesel. There was also a 550 version that used a Daihatsu 548cc, three-cylinder engine.

Lancia

Fabbrica Automobili Lancia e Cia SpA was founded by Vincenzo Lancia and Claudio Fogolin in 1906. By 1911, Lancia had become a major Italian auto maker, offering a wide range of passenger cars as well as commercial vehicles up through large diesels and buses.

1939-53 Lancia Ardea

Lancia unveiled the legendary Aprilia in 1937, the last car designed by Vincenzo Lancia. In 1939, Lancia brought out the Ardea whose styling faithfully followed the Aprilia. This was the first Lancia with a displacement of under 1ltr. The 903cc, 29hp V-4 was able to get as much as 40mpg, and the 1,650lb Ardea had a top speed of 67mph. Like the Aprilia, there was a fully independent suspension system with a semi-elliptic leaf spring, torsion bars, and trailing arms in the rear. Like all Lancias up through 1956, and for some models through 1963, there was a sliding pillar suspension up front. When fitted with a five-speed gearbox in 1949, Lancia claimed a first. Ardea sold well with over 22,000 built.

'39-53 Ardea 4-door sedan

Chapter 6

Japan

The early postwar Japanese cars were spartan and simple to keep prices affordable, and even then a new car often cost as much as a Japanese home. Very poor roads meant that cars had to be rugged. They did not need to be able to travel very fast. There were special incentives for tiny cars, including financial aid to companies building vehicles with small displacement engines. The *Kei Jidoski* microcar class put limits on size—3m long, 1.3m wide, and 2m high.

The tax structure favored "midget" cars with under 360cc engines being much lower than "small" cars with 361cc to 2000cc engines. As a further incentive, midget cars were exempted from obligatory and quite expensive periodic overhauls. In cities, owners of midget cars did not have to prove that they had a place to park their cars before they could buy them. Of the 294,000 cars built in 1960, nearly 56 percent were midgets. This dropped to about 25 percent by the end of the 1960s and only 3 percent by the mid-1980s. In 1976, the displacement for the midget class was increased to 550cc.

Daihatsu

While the Hatsudoki Seizo Kaisha Company was formed in 1907 to produce engines, vehicles were not built until 1930. These were motorcycle-type, commercial three-wheelers with handlebars. There were name changes to Daihatsu Kogyo Kabushiki Kaisha in 1951 and Daihatsu Motor Company, Ltd., in 1974. Daihatsu's first car, the 1958 four-door Bee, was also a three-wheeler powered by a 540cc, rear-mounted, two-cylinder engine. Few were built. By the 1970s, Daihatsu was a major auto maker. By 1968, Daihatsu was part of Toyota, and some Toyota models were sold as badge-engineered Daihatsus.

1963-68 Compagno

The Compagno, Daihatsu's first four-wheel car, had a four-cylinder, 797cc, 41hp,

One of about a dozen Daihatsu Tri-Mobile trucks with a 305cc motorcycle engine that were imported into the United States. This 1962 van is owned by Dick Strange. *Bill Siuru*

'63-68 Compagno sedan/ station wagon	★★★
'63-68 Compagno roadster	★★★★
'66-75 Fellow/Fellow Max sedan/station wagon	★★★
'69-76 Consorte sedan/coupe	★★
'76-93 Cuore/Mira	★★
'77-93 Charade coupe/ sedan/hatchback	★★
add one star for turbocharged or 4WD versions	

water-cooled engine mounted in front with rear-wheel drive. The Compagno came as a two-door sedan, station wagon, and two-seat sports roadster. The displacement was increased to 958cc in 1965 for the 1000 series with 55hp in sedans and station wagons. In the sport version, a twin-barrel carburetor increased power to 65hp. Other features included a fully synchronized four-speed and a rigid rear axle with semi-elliptic leaf springs. Fuel injection and front disc brakes were offered after 1967.

1966-75 Fellow/Fellow Max

The Fellow, Daihatsu's entry in the 360cc market, had a water-cooled, twin-cylinder, 356cc, two-stroke, 23hp engine. It came as a two-door sedan and station wagon. A second redesigned series, called the Fellow Max, appeared in 1970. Depending on the model, horsepower was either 31 or 37 from the twin-cylinder engine. Available in either sedan or coupe form, the Fellow Max had front-wheel drive, a fully synchronized four-speed, and four-wheel independent suspension.

1969-76 Consorte

The front-engine, rear-wheel-drive Consorte replacement for the Compagno came out in 1969 and shared much with the contemporary Toyota Corolla. Engines included a 958cc, 58hp, four-cylinder and a 1166cc unit with 64hp. These powerplants were also used in the Corolla. The 1166cc version had disc brakes in front and a five-speed transmission; Toyo-Glide automatic was an option. While the front suspension was independent, the rear was a rigid axle with semileaf springs. Besides sedans, there was a five-passenger coupe.

1976-93 Cuore/Mira

The 1976 Cuore was developed from the Fellow Max and was powered by a new two-cylinder, four-stroke, 574cc, 58hp water-cooled engine. This front-wheel-drive car with a transversely mounted engine was sold in some markets as the Domino. There was a complete body restyling for 1980, and the Mira version debuted. An optional turbocharged engine boosted output to 41hp, and for some markets, there was a 617cc engine. Transmissions included a four-speed, five-speed, or a two-speed automatic. In a four-wheel-drive version, power was supplied to the rear wheels as well. By 1985, there was a third generation Cuore/Mira with a three-cylinder, 840cc, 44hp engine and was available either as a three- or five-door hatchback.

1977-93 Charade

The Charade sedan appeared in 1977, and the coupe came out in 1978. The 993cc engine was a three-cylinder with 50 or 55hp. When a revised version appeared in 1983, horsepower was up to 60. The Charade de Tomaso Turbo used turbocharging to achieve 80hp; there were also two diesel 993cc models that made 38hp and 50hp with a turbocharger. A major redesign in 1985 featured more aerodynamic styling. When Charades began appearing in the United States in the late 1980s, they were fitted with a 993cc, 53hp, three-cylinder engine or an optional 1295cc, 80hp, four-cylinder engine. There were disc/drum brakes, a MacPherson strut/coil spring suspension in front, a rigid rear axle with coil springs, and either a five-speed or automatic transmission. By the 1980s, and depending on the market, Charades were available as four-door sedans or hatchbacks with either three or five doors.

Hino

Hino Motors, Ltd., founded in 1942, got into auto making in 1953 as a sideline to its commercial vehicle business. Besides small cars, Hino offered Humbee three-wheel, handlebar-steered trucks. Toyota acquired Hino in 1965, and by 1967, car production ceased.

'53-61 4CV 4-door sedan	★★★
'61-64 Contessa 900 4-door sedan	★★★
'62-64 Contessa 900 2-door coupe	★★★★

1953-67 4CV and Contessa 900

Hino built the Renault 4CV under license, and, except for right-hand drive, it was modified little from the French version. This was followed by the Contessa 900 which evolved from the 4CV and resembled the Renault Dauphine. Hino's four-cylinder engine was slightly larger at 893cc and 35hp.

Hinos began to take on their own look when Italy's Michelotti designed a coupe around the Contessa 900. Its rear engine was tweaked to produce 45hp. Hino also produced the Briska pickups that used the 893cc engine. Hino continued to build cars until 1967, but these were larger Contessa 1300s using a 1251cc engine, though still rear-mounted.

Honda

As auto makers go, Honda is a relative newcomer. Soichiro Honda did not start building cars until 1962. By then, Honda Motor Company, Ltd., was the world's largest motorcycle manufacturer.

1963-70 S-500/S-600/S-800

The initial Honda cars were two-seat, open-top sports cars that debuted in October 1962 at the Tokyo Motor Show. When production started in 1963, the first model was the S-500 roadster with a 531cc four-cylinder engine. This twin-cam, water-cooled engine produced 44hp at a motorcycle-like 8000-rpm. Top speed was 80mph.

The drivetrain showed a definite motorcycle heritage. The four-speed transmission was synchronized on the top three ratios and was located between the seats. This was linked to a differential behind the seats via a short driveshaft. The differential, in turn, was connected to the rear wheels by a twin chain drive. There was a fully independent suspension with unequal length wishbones, ball joints, longitudinal torsion bars, and double-action telescopic shock absorbers up front.

While successful in France, Hino's 4CV turned out to be a bit fragile for the poor Japanese roads of the era. *Toyota*

'63-64 S-500 roadster	★★★★
'64-66 S-600 roadster	★★★★★
'65-66 S-600 coupe	★★★★
'66-70 S-800 roadster	★★★★★
'66-70 S-800 coupe	★★★★★
'66-72 N-360/N-400/N-500/ N-600 2-door sedan	★★★
'71-72 Z 360/600 2-door coupe	★★★
'71-73 Life 360 4-door sedan	★★

The S-600 used a 606cc engine that produced 57hp at 8500rpm; it pushed the 1,575lb S-600 to 90mph. After 1965, the relatively tall aluminum, four-cylinder, dohc engine was slanted to clear the low hood line. The S-600 came in both roadster and fastback coupe form; both were two-seaters.

The S800 came in both roadster and

The 1961-64 Hino 900 still showed its Renault heritage, looking a bit like the Renault Dauphine. *Toyota*

With an overall length of 130in and a 79in wheelbase, the Honda S600 was slightly smaller than the contemporary Austin-Healey Sprite and MG Midget. This S600 is owned by Brian Baker. *Brian Baker*

1966-73 Honda 360/N-600, Z Coupe, and Life

Honda had joined the hot Japanese 360cc market with its N360 minicar. It featured a 354cc, 31hp, two-cylinder engine driving the front wheels. When Honda entered the American market in late 1969, it upgraded the Honda 360 by switching to a 598cc engine to create the N-600. Relying on its motorcycle experience, the powerplant was a vertical, overhead-cam, air-cooled twin. The engine produced 35-45hp.

Other mechanical features on the N-600 sedan included front disc/rear drum brakes, rack and pinion steering, front MacPherson struts with coil springs, and a rigid rear axle with semi-elliptic leaf springs. The standard transmission had four forward gears with a shifter projecting out beneath the dashboard. A three-speed Hondamatic was optional. While not offered in the United States, there was also an N-400 with a 401cc, 33hp twin and an N-500 with a 497cc, 40hp engine.

When it came to performance, the most impressive figure was the 35–40mpg fuel economy; this gave the car well over 200 miles from the 6.9gal fuel tank. Top speed was 75-80mph.

In 1971, the N-600 sedan was joined by the Z coupe. While using the same mechanics, the coupe had a more "sporty" body. The coupe was a couple of inches shorter in both length and height compared to the

fastback coupe form. Besides a displacement increase to 791cc, there was a switch to a more conventional hypoid bevel, solid rear end, though 1966 S800s did retain the chain drive. The new rear axle set-up was located by four trailing arms and a Panhard rod. Coil springs over tube shocks were used. As before, there was a stout ladder frame. Engine output was 70hp; top speed was 100mph. Honda touted the S-800 as the fastest under-1ltr sports car in the world. Honda built 26,587 of these tiny sports cars, of which about 14,241 were S800 roadsters and coupes.

The Honda 600 was a pretty efficient package considering it was a four-passenger sedan that was only 125in long with a 78.75in wheelbase. The unitized body helped keep the car's weight under 1,400lb, and it rolled on tiny 5.20x10 tires. *Honda*

Many minicar and microcar enthusiasts do not take their cars that seriously. This Honda 600 coupe is used to tow an Isetta converted to electric power. *Bill Siuru*

N600 sedan. Top speed was a couple mph more because of the coupe's somewhat better aerodynamics.

The coupe was a four-passenger car in name only, though the rear hatch and fold-down rear seat made for a utilitarian "city car." The coupe also got 145SR10 tires, a tachometer, and an aircraft-overhead light console. Other features included a fully synchronized four-speed transmission and front disc brakes. The coupe was also offered with a 354cc engine tweaked to give 36hp in a TS version. The Life three- and five-door hatchbacks, debuting in 1971, used the 356cc, 30hp, water-cooled, two-cylinder engine, an independent front suspension, and a live rear axle. The Life introduced the styling of the Honda Civic, Honda's first highly successful four-wheeler on the American market.

Mazda

The Toyo Cork Kogyo Company was established in 1920 to manufacture cork products and machinery. By 1923, it was building small motorcycles, then shifted to motorcycle-based, three-wheel trucks. The first product to use the Mazda name was the 1931 DA three-wheel truck. After the war, production resumed with three-wheel trucks, and, by 1950, four-wheel trucks as well.

1960-66 R-360, P-360/P-600 Carol

The Mazda R-360 was Toyo Kogyo's first production automobile. The tiny two-seat coupe was powered by a rear-mounted, air-cooled, 356cc, 16hp, twin-cylinder V engine. Besides the standard four-speed, the R-360 could be ordered with an optional automatic. The coupe used an independent suspension system. Top speed for such a tiny car was an impressive 65mph. Equally impressive was the claimed 94mpg.

By 1962, Mazda was producing the four-seat Carol with an air-cooled, 358cc, 20hp, four-cylinder engine mounted transversely in the rear. The Carol was available either as a two- or four-door sedan and had a top speed of 65mph. The P-360 Carol was very popular, capturing 67 percent of the Japanese midget car market. In 1964, the Carol got a 586cc,

The 1960 R-360 was Mazda's first car. It was quite popular with 23,417 sold in the first year. *Mazda*

'60-62 R-360 2-door coupe	★★★★
'62-66 P-360/P-600 Carol 2- and 4-door sedan	★★★
'64-69 Familia 800/1000 2- and 4-door sedan, station wagon	★★★

28hp engine, and the model was designated the P-600. The four-stroke, water-cooled engine was also transversely mounted.

1964-69 Familia 800/1000

Mazda moved a bit upscale with the Familia. The Familia 800 had its 782cc, 45hp, four-cylinder, water-cooled engine mounted up front. Top speed was 71mph. There were a sedan, coupe, and later a two-door station wagon. Either a four-speed manual gearbox or two-speed automatic transmission was available. The Familia 1000 used a 985cc, 68hp engine that boosted the top speed to 90mph.

Mazda competed in the Japanese micro-car market with cars like the Chantez, which appeared in 1972. The Chantez featured a 359cc, 35hp, water-cooled, two-cylinder, front-mounted engine. It also had front-wheel drive and a fully synchronized four-speed transmission.

Mitsubishi

Mitsubishi goes back to the 1870s and the Mitsubishi Shokai shipbuilding company. Mitsubishi built its first car, the Model A, in 1917; it was greatly influenced by the

In 1989, Mazda began offering the modern-looking Autozam Carol microcar mainly for the home market. *Mazda*

Fiat Tipo Zero. While only about twenty cars were built, the Model A is often credited with being the first Japanese car built by a major company to see "series" production. Mitsubishi got into auto making by assembling Kaiser's Henry Js and Jeeps in the 1950s. In 1971, the Mitsubishi Motor Corporation began its long association with Chrysler.

1960-63 Mitsubishi A-10/500 and Super Deluxe

Mitsubishi's first car was a tiny—only 118in long—two-door, four-seat sedan that was developed in response to government encouragement to build a "people's" car. The A-10 was also known as the 500 because of its rear-mounted, air-cooled, twin-cylinder, four-stroke, 493cc, 21hp at 5000rpm engine. With its suicide doors, rounded fenders, and minimal trim, the A-10 was hardly a beauty. Indeed, it looked a bit like the German Gogomobil. The 500 did have a fully independent suspension, drum brakes, a three-speed gearbox, and a 56mph top

'60-63 A10/500/Super Deluxe 2-door sedan	★★★★
'62-64 Colt 600 2-door sedan	★★★
'63-69 Colt 1000/1100 4-door sedan	★★★
'64-70 Colt 800/1000F/11F 2-door hatchback	★★★
'62-69 Minica 2-door sedan and station wagon	★★★
'70-84 Minica F4 and Ami 55	★★

speed. In 1961, a Super Deluxe model was added. This used a 594cc, 25hp engine. The top speed was still 56mph.

1962-70 Colt 600, 800, 1000, 1000F, 1100, and 11F

The Model 500 evolved into the Colt 600 with styling changes that improved the looks markedly. While improved, it still carried cues from the A10, including the suicide-type doors and fender scoops for the rear-mounted engine. The two-door Colt 600 sedan had an 81in wheelbase, 134in overall length, and 62mph top speed. The 600 used an 594cc, 25hp engine.

In 1963, a restyled and larger Colt 1000 appeared. The new Colt was 152in long and had a 90in wheelbase. The four-door sedan used a four-cylinder, 977cc, 51hp engine, which was now mounted up front. In 1966, a new 1088cc, four-cylinder engine was installed in the four-door sedan for the Colt 1100. The Colt 1100S was a sporty variant that included a floor-shifted, four-speed transmission and a tachometer.

In 1964, Mitsubishi brought out the Colt 800 three-door fastback. Most interesting was the three-cylinder, water-cooled, two-stroke, 843cc, 45hp engine. This was a surprising and rather unsuccessful move, since the main proponent of this engine configuration, Saab, was phasing it out. The Colt 800 was a relatively small vehicle with an overall length of 144in. By 1966, the engine was replaced by a more conventional 1000cc, four-cylinder, four-stroke engine in the Colt 1000F. Besides the three-door version, there was now a five-door one. The last model to use the somewhat unpopular fastback was the 1968 11F with a 1088cc engine. In the final version, the engine was tuned to produce 73hp.

1962-84 Minica 360, Minica F4, and Ami 55

The long-running Minica series started out with the Minica 360. Available as either a sedan or station wagon, the first Minica used a 359cc, two-stroke, air-cooled, 18hp engine and a four-speed transmission. While the front suspension was independent, there was a rigid axle suspended by semi-elliptic springs in the rear. This resulted in a rugged but stiff ride. The Minica proved popular in rural areas but not urban ones. Top speed was 55mph.

The Minica was revised in 1969 with sedans, vans, and a Skipper coupe available. Initially, the 30hp engine was air-cooled but was superseded by a 38hp water-cooled, two-cylinder, four-cycle engine for the F4 series to meet more stringent emission requirements. Also, coil springs replaced the leaf springs in the rear. This model was followed by the Ami 55, which used a 546cc, 31hp engine in the body. Top speed was in the range of 68 to 75mph. By 1984, the Minica series, now labeled the Econo, had acquired front-wheel drive with its 546cc, ohc, three-valve-per-cylinder engine transversely mounted in front. The engine produced 31hp in basic form and 39hp when turbocharged. Top speeds were 68mph and 71mph, respectively.

Nissan and Datsun

Nissan traces its history back to 1912 when American-trained Japanese engineer, Masujiro Hashimoto, founded the Kwaishinsha Motor Car Works. Hashimoto's partners in the venture were Kenjiro Den, Rokuro Aoyama, and Meitaro Takeuchi, their initials spelling DAT. It marketed its first car in 1915. By 1931, it was producing small cars, essentially Austin Seven clones, under the Datson label, or son of DAT. Since "Datson" sounded too much like "to lose money" or "ruin" in Japanese, the name was changed to Datsun. "Sun" was the symbol of the emerging Japanese Empire.

The small Datsuns went through a succession of models—Type 10, 12, 14, 15, 16, and 17—with styling changes but still used basically the same Austin-based mechanics. Production reached 15,000 units in 1937, but manufacture of Datsun cars ceased the following year.

After World War II, Nissan returned, building warmed-over prewar models and British Austin A40s and A50s under license. The 1951 Thrift (DS2, 4, 5, etc.) two-doors and four-doors got new slab-sided body designs that were almost trucklike. The Thrift models were powered by a somewhat larger 860cc, but still British-inspired, engine.

'52-54 DC-3 roadster	★★★★★
'55-58 Type 110 4-door sedan/ station wagon	★★★
'58-60 PL210 (1000) 4-door sedan	★★★
'59-61 SPL211/SPL212/ SPL313 roadster	★★★★★

1955-58 Type 110

Still relecting a British influence, at least mechanically, the Type 110 had a 860cc, four-cylinder, 25hp engine and a column-shifted, four-speed, fully synchronized transmission. The styling was still chunky with lines only slightly less boxy than the previous Thrift models. A conventional channel-section chassis was used with rigid axles and semi-elliptic springs front and rear. Top speed was 53mph, and the line-up included an equally boxy looking K110 convertible, plus a station wagon and pickup.

1952-69 Datsun Sports Cars

Nissan was the first Japanese auto maker to produce a sports car after the war. The 1952 DC-3 Datsun Sport used the 860cc, water-cooled, L-head, four-cylinder engine that produced a mere 25hp. With its fender-mounted headlamps, cut-down doors, and fold-down windshield, it resembled a shrunken MG T-Type. Using a nonsynchronized three-speed transmission, rigid leaf-spring suspension, and having a top speed of only 43mph, it was far from exciting. The DC-3 was built for the home market where bone-jarring ruggedness to withstand war-ravaged highways was still more important than speed and good handling.

The next Nissan sports car was the 1959 SPL211. Power came from a 988cc, 34hp, four-cylinder engine, and top speed jumped to 71mph. This four-passenger roadster featured a fiberglass body but still had a rigid suspension system. This was followed by the SPL212 and SPL213 in 1960 and 1961, respectively. These were basically the same car with a 1189cc, ohv, four-cylinder engine producing 48hp in the SPL212 and 60hp in the SPL213.

These early sports cars gave Nissan the experience to develop the sports car that

The Datsun SPL211 bore more than a passing resemblance to the British Austin-Healey 100 right down to the two-tone paint scheme. *Nissan*

caught the attention of the enthusiast—the Datsun 1600 and 2000 roadsters and, of course, the 240Z.

1958-60 PL210 (1000)

The Type 210 that appeared in 1958 still used quite boxy styling and the 988cc, 34hp engine. The column-shifted, four-speed transmission was synchronized on the top three gears. The body rode on a pressed, box-section, 87.4in wheelbase chassis and was 152in long. Longer wheelbase PL211 and PL221 sedans were also produced. Rigid axles with semi-elliptic leaf springs were used in both front and rear. This was the first Datsun model to appear in the United States, where it was sold as the Datsun 1000 with a slightly more powerful 37hp version of the 988cc engine.

Nissan has never been a contender in the Japanese microcar market. However, it has offered numerous models with a just-under-1ltr engine, often the base engine with other larger displacement engines available. Examples include the 1965-69 Sunny B10, the 1970-78 Cherry, Nissan's first front-wheel-drive car, and the 1982-90 March/Micra, available with 988cc plus larger engines. The 1989 Nissan Pao, based on the March/Micra, was nostalgically styled like the microcars of the past but featured a body made of synthetic materials and a 988cc engine.

Subaru

Fuji Heavy Industries, Ltd., Subaru's parent, evolved from the Nakajima Aircraft Company that was dismantled at the end of World War II. While founded in 1953, car building only began in 1958 with the Subaru 360 minicar.

1958-70 360, Maia, and Young S/SS

The Subaru 360 was one of the earliest and most successful of the 360cc class of Japanese microcars. The 360 used an air-cooled, two-cylinder, 356cc, two-stroke engine placed transversely in the rear. It produced 16hp but was increased to 20hp in 1964. A three-speed transmission was fitted initially, but a four-speed became available by 1964. Mechanical brakes were used through the mid-1960s, then replaced by hydraulic ones, and tires were tiny 4.80x10s. Overall length was 118in with a 70.9in wheelbase. The fully independent suspension system used trailing arms, torsion bars, and coil springs in front and split semi-axles and torsion bars in the rear.

There were many variations on the 360 platform besides the basic two-door sedan. The 1959-64 Subaru 360 convertible was really a sedan with a large sunroof that rolled back down to the rear deck lid. Actually, the 1959-62 "folding utility sedan" was more of a convertible, since here the rear half of the roof was canvas, and the area behind the doors and above the beltline folded down for

'58-70 360 2-door sedan	★★★
'59-70 360 2-door utility/ custom sedan	★★★★
'59-64 360 2-door convertible	★★★★
'60-66 Maia/450 2-door sedan	★★★
'68-70 360 Young S and SS 2-door sedan	★★★★
'69-72 R-2 2-door sedan	★★★
'70-72 R-2 SS and GSS	★★★★
'70-71 R-2 Sporty DX and L	★★★★
'72-90 Rex, Rex 5, and Rex 550	★★
'66-71 FF-1 1000/1100 2/4-door sedan and 2/4-door wagon	★★
'83-95 Justy 3/4 door hatchback	★
add one star for turbocharged and 4WD Rex	
add one star for 4WD Justy	

In 1968, Malcolm Bricklin, of Bricklin and Yugo fame, began importing the Subaru 360 into the United States. These had a 25hp engine plus four-speed transmission and hydraulic brakes. The 360's biggest selling point was its list price of a mere $1,297. They sold very poorly. *Subaru*

carrying tall objects or tall people. The utility sedan was replaced in 1963 by the Custom, a squareback-sedan that provided a bit more headroom for the rear seat passengers. Starting in 1961, Subaru offered a number of differ-ent minivan and van-like truck models, based on the 360 mechanics, in its Sambar series.

There were even special versions of the sedan, like the Maia and Young editions. The 1960-66 Maia, or 450, used the 360 sedan

Subaru also produced a series of trucks and vans on the 360 platform. This nice example belongs to Ed Parsil. *Ed Parsil*

The Subaru 360 Young S featured an upscale interior including a padded dash, leather-wrapped steering wheel, and better instrumentation including a tachometer. *Bill Siuru*

The R-2 replaced the 360. This is the "higher-performance" SS version. The 1970-71 R-2 SS and

1971-72 R-2 GSS replaced the Young SS using the same 36hp powerplant. *Subaru*

body but was powered by a larger 423cc engine that produced 23hp, allowing a 62mph top speed compared to the basic 360's 50-plus mph. The Young S, for "Sport," featured an upscale interior, and the engine produced 25hp. Externally, there were tubular bumpers and distinctive "YOUNG" trim items. The ultimate Subaru was the Young SS, or Super Sport, with the 360cc engine using twin carburetors. Top speed for the Young SS was 75mph.

1969-72 R-2

The 360 platform was totally redesigned, given an updated body without suicide doors, and renamed the R-2. The 356cc, two-cylinder engine was rated at 30hp, and there was a fully synchronized four-speed gearbox. Besides the base two-door sedan, there was a squareback sedan, as well as truck and van versions. The upscale 1970-71 Sporty DX and 1971-72 L had a couple more horsepower. There were also SS and GSS "high-performance" versions of the R-2.

1972-90 Rex, Rex 5, and Rex 550

While the more modern Rex replacement for the R-2 still had the two-cylinder, 356cc engine, it now was water-cooled and became a four-stroke in 1973 with 358cc and 28hp. This grew to 490cc with 31hp for the Rex 5 in 1976; the 1977 Rex 550 had 544cc, still with 31hp, but with more torque. The Rex series was revised in 1981 with three- and five-door hatchbacks available. Again, the 544cc twin was used, but by 1984, there was a turbocharged version with 41hp at 6000rpm. The Rex 700 was also available with a 665cc, 37hp engine, and after 1983, there was a four-wheel-drive version of the Rex 550. There was another styling revision in 1986 for the three- and five-door hatchbacks. There were also corresponding trucks and minivans, including four-wheel-drive versions of the latter.

1966-71 FF-1 Star, 1000, and 1100

In 1966, Subaru started building a more conventional car with a four-cylinder engine up front driving the front wheels. Initially, it

The Subaru Rex five-door hatchback of the late 1980s. *Subaru*

appeared as the 1000 with a 977cc, horizontally opposed, water-cooled engine producing 55hp. This was the first use of the "boxer" style engines that would become a Subaru trademark. By 1969, the engine had grown to 1098cc for the FF-1 Star or Subaru 1100, which remained in production through 1971. The FF-1 Star series featured a 95.2in wheelbase and a 155in overall length on the two- and four-door sedans and 153in on the two- and four-door station wagons. The four-wheel independent suspension used wishbones with torsion bars in front and trailing arms and torsion bars in the rear. The replacement Leone series appeared in 1971 with several engines, starting with the 1098cc unit.

1983-95 Justy

The Justy used a 997cc, 55hp, three-cylinder, ohc, water-cooled engine mounted up front and driving the front wheels. It came as either a three- or five-door hatchback on a 90in wheelbase with an overall length of 139in. When introduced into the United States as a 1987 model, it was fitted with a 1189cc, 66hp version of the three-cylinder engine. Both front-wheel-drive and

four-wheel-drive versions were offered. The Justy was restyled in 1989, replacing the earlier boxy looks with more rounded lines and a 6in longer length.

Suzuki

The Suzuki Loom Works was founded in 1909 by Michio Suzuki. While a few prototype

The front-wheel-drive Subaru FF-1 with its flat-four engine was a more conventional car. When fitted with a 1267cc engine, the 1300 version helped Subaru gain a serious foothold in the United States. *Subaru*

Initially, the Justy came with a five-speed gearbox, but, in 1989, it was available with an electronic continuously variable transmission ECVT built under license from Van Doorne in Holland. ECVT was also available on the Rex series. *Subaru*

cars with 750cc engines were built in the 1930s, Suzuki did not start building cars in quantity until the early 1960s.

1955-67 Suzulight Series

Suzuki's first model was the 1955 Suzulight that looked much like the German Lloyd, not surprising since Suzuki obtained Volkswagens, Citroens, and Lloyds during its development. Like the Lloyd, it had a front-mounted, two-stroke, two-cylinder, air-cooled, 360cc engine. Only forty-three Suzulights were built.

While introduced in the 1950s, serious production of the Suzulight 360 did not start until 1962 when 2,565 were built. Again, a 360cc, air-cooled, 21hp, twin-cylinder engine was used, but now in a more modern, though boxy, two-door body on a backbone chassis. Other features included drum brakes, and the four-wheel independent suspension used transverse leaf springs on both axles. Top

speed was 53mph. Small vans and pickups were also built on the same platform.

1967-82 Fronte 360, LC 10, LC 50, and Cervo

In 1967, the Suzulight 360 was replaced by the Fronte 360, or LC 10, with an updated body. Now an air-cooled, two-stroke, three-cylinder, 360cc engine was rear-mounted and drove the rear wheels. The engine produced 25hp in base form and 36hp in the three-carbureted SS model; top speeds were 68mph and 78mph for the SS.

The Suzuki minicar series was updated in 1970 with the Fronte LC 50, which used the same mechanics but in a totally new body. Depending on the model, the rear-mounted, 360cc, three-cylinder engine produced 31 to 36hp. Water-cooled engines were introduced in 1974, and Suzuki's first four-stroke engine came in 1977. In 1976, a slightly larger 443cc engine was offered. A

'55-56 Suzulight 2-door sedan	★★★★★
'59-67 Suzulight 360 2-door sedan	★★★
'64-69 Fronte 800 2/4-door sedan	★★★
'67-69 Fronte 360/LC 10 2-door sedan	★★★
'70-78 Fronte LC 50	★★★
'77-90 Cervo 2-door coupe	★★★
'79-90 Fronte Alto	★★
'83-95 Cultus/Swift/Sprint/ Firefly/Metro	★★
'90-93 Geo Metro convertible	★★★
add one star for turbo version	

rather attractive fastback Cervo coupe with a 539cc engine was added to the line-up in 1977. The original rear-engined Cervo coupe design remained in production until 1981 while the sedan was replaced by the all-new Fronte Alto in 1979. The Cervo coupe was also offered with a four-cylinder, 970cc engine in some markets.

1979-90 Fronte Alto and Cervo

The 1979 Fronte Alto was a very up-to-date minicar with front-wheel drive, and its four-stroke, 547cc, three-cylinder, 31hp engine mounted transversely up front. The two-stroke, 539cc engine was still offered for a while. The Cervo coupe was likewise revised for front-wheel drive in 1982, and, by 1983, the 547cc engine was turbocharged to produce 40hp at 6000rpm in the Cervo de Tomaso version. Other variants included an Alto three-door hatchback, Fronte five-door hatchback, Mighty Boy pickup, four-wheel-drive version, and a performance-oriented Alto Works Twincam RS-R that obtained 45hp (63hp with turbocharger). A 796cc, 40hp, overhead camshaft, three-cylinder engine was also available after 1981.

1964-69 Fronte 800

The Fronte 800 sedan appeared as a slightly larger, more luxurious alternative to the Suzulight 360 series. Power came from a front-mounted, three-cylinder, two-stroke, 785cc, 41hp engine driving the front wheels. Other features included unit body construction, a fully independent suspension, drum brakes, a fully synchronized four-speed transmission, and a 75mph top speed.

1983-95 Cultus, Swift, Sprint, Firefly, and Geo Metro

An all-new Suzuki ultra-economy car grew out of a 1981 agreement among Suzuki, General Motors, and Isuzu. The result was a three- or five-door front-wheel-drive hatchback that had either a 993cc, 48 to 50hp, three-cylinder engine or a four-cylinder, 1324cc, 66 to 72hp engine. A turbocharged version of the three-cylinder powerplant was rated at 80hp. Other specifications included a McPherson strut front suspension, a rigid rear axle, and either a five-speed manual or a three-speed automatic transmission. The cars were sold as the Suzuki Cultus in Japan, the Suzuki Swift in some markets, and the Chevrolet Sprint in the United States. There was also a Pontiac Firefly for Canadian buyers. By 1989, the Chevrolet version was marketed as the Geo Metro with either the three-cylinder, 999cc engine or a 1.3ltr, four-cylinder engine.

Toyota

Just before the turn of the century, Sakichi Toyoda invented many major improvements for weaving looms. Funds from sales of these patents allowed son Kiichiro Toyoda to get into the automobile business. Prewar Toyotas were highly influenced by cars such as the Chrysler Airflow, Chevrolet, and Volvo PV60.

1947-53 S-Series (SA, SC, SD, SF)

The Model SA, appearing in 1947, was a much smaller car and borrowed virtually

'47-52 SA 2-door sedan	★★★★★
'49-53 SC/SD/SF 4-door sedan	★★★★
'57-60 Corona ST10/PT10/PT20 4-door sedan	★★★
'61-78 Publica/1000 2-door sedan	★★★
'62-64 Publica pickup/station wagon	★★★
'62-64 Publica convertible	★★★★
'64-69 Sport 800	★★★★★

The Toyota SD was part of the S-series, Toyota's first small cars, which were in production between 1947 and 1953. *Toyota*

nothing from the prewar Toyotas. The two-door sedan with suicide doors was powered by a four-cylinder, 997cc, 27hp engine. It featured a backbone chassis and coil spring suspension. Production did not really start until 1949, and only about 215 SAs were built.

The Model SA was the first of a series of four-door sedans that included the Model SC, SD, and SF which remained in production until 1953. The SF was the most popular with 3,653 produced between 1951 and 1953. The Toyota RH Super, brought out in 1953 and in production until 1955, used the SF body but with a larger 1453cc, 48hp, four-cylinder engine.

1957-60 Corona

The first Toyota Corona ST10 appeared in 1957 and had a four-cylinder, 995cc, 33hp engine. With a 154in overall length, a 94.5in wheelbase, and weighing over 2,100, it was no lightweight. This was followed in 1959 by the PT10, which used a revised 997cc engine. In 1960, there was the completely restyled PT20 with a somewhat more powerful version of the 997cc engine.

The ST20's revised suspension, featuring torsion bars in front and a cantilever setup in the rear, reflected the higher speeds now possible on improved Japanese roads as well as a demand for a smoother ride. Toyota built over 41,000 of these small-engined Coronas, 25,000 PT20s in 1960 alone. With the substitution of a 1453cc, 60hp engine in 1961, the Corona moved out of the minicar range.

1961-69 Publica

The Publica series was initially aimed at the home market. The initial 700 designation denoted the car's 697cc, two-cylinder, air-cooled, 28hp engine. This grew to 790cc and 40hp. When fitted with a 933cc, 58hp, four-cylinder engine, it was called the 1000 and became an export model. There was also a 1166cc, 68hp version. From 1962, there were station wagons, convertibles, and pickups, in addition to sedans.

The Publica/1000 was continued through 1978 with some 1,350,000 built over an eighteen-year period before being superseded by

When the Corona "grew up," it was replaced by the Publica series. This version was fitted with a 790cc engine. *Toyota*

While most Publicas were sedans, there were other rarer models, like this rather handsome convertible of 1962-64 vintage. *Toyota*

The star of the Publica series was the Sport 800 coupe that appeared in 1965. Its 760cc, 45hp engine could push the aerodynamically designed two-seater to a top speed of 96mph. A total of 3,120 Sport 800s had been built when production ceased in 1969. *Toyota*

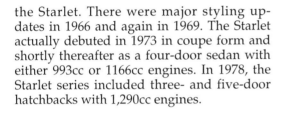

the Starlet. There were major styling updates in 1966 and again in 1969. The Starlet actually debuted in 1973 in coupe form and shortly thereafter as a four-door sedan with either 993cc or 1166cc engines. In 1978, the Starlet series included three- and five-door hatchbacks with 1,290cc engines.

Chapter 7

Netherlands and Sweden

DAF

DAF's biggest claim to fame was that it was the first minicar to have a true automatic transmission as standard equipment. Indeed, the DAF came about mainly because of the continuously variable transmission (CVT) invented by Hubert Jozef van Doorne. He and his brother, Wim, operated Van Doorne's Automobielfabriek (DAF) NV, in the Netherlands, a major producer of heavy-duty commercial vehicles.

DAF's CVT, called Variomatic, provided an unlimited range of gear ratios and clutchless driving. Variomatic eliminated gear shifting completely with only a simple "Drive" or "Reverse" lever needed. This made the DAF one of the easiest cars to

'58-61 600 2-door sedan	★★★
'61-63 750/Type 30 2-door sedan	★★★
'63-65 DAFfodil Type 31 2-door sedan	★★★
'66-67 DAFfodil Type 32 2-door sedan	★★★
'67-74 DAF 33 2-door sedan	★★★
'66-74 DAF 44 2-door sedan	★★★
'67-72 DAF 55 2-door sedan	★★★
'72-76 DAF 66 2-door sedan	★★★
'74-76 DAF 46 2-door sedan	★★★
'76-78 Volvo 66 2-door sedan	★★★

add one star for pickup, van, combi, station wagon, and coupe

The first DAF Type 600 was a unit-bodied, two-door sedan with an overall length of 142in and 81in wheelbase. The 600 could hold five in a pinch. *Kaz Wysocki*

drive. CVT, with improvements, has been offered, for example, in the Subaru Justy ECVT, Fiat Uno Selectra, and the Ford Fiesta and Escort CTX.

During the years of production, 1960-75, well over 800,000 DAFs of all types had been built.

1958-61 DAF 600 (Type 22)

The first DAF was the 600, or Type 22, with a very BMW-like two-cylinder, horizontally opposed, air-cooled, 590cc, 22hp engine. Variomatic used in the 600 provided

Only trim changes distinguished the 750 externally from the 600. *Kazmier Wysocki*

The 1967-74 DAF 33 received a facelift, and, after 1972, had electric controls for the Variomatic transmission. *A. Meyer*

an infinite number of gear ratios, from 20:1 for initial acceleration, to 4.4:1 for cruising. Zero to 50mph acceleration took a leisurely 41.5 seconds, and top speed was around 55mph. Fuel economy was 40mpg. Like all DAFs to come, the 600 had a fully independent suspension system. Up front there was a traverse leaf spring and the hydraulic shock absorbers serving as swivels. In the rear there were independent swing half axles with pivoting V-shaped control arms with triangular guides and coil springs. Smallish 7in diameter drum brakes and 5.20x12 tires were used on a package that weighed less than 1,400lb. Some 30,563 DAF 600s were built, including 440 pickups.

1961-74 DAF 750, DAFfodil Type 30, 31 and 32, and DAF 33

The DAF 750's two-cylinder engine was increased to 746cc and 30hp. The 750 was able to hit 70mph and still provide 32 to 40mpg. Ratios for the Variomatic transmission now went from 3.9:1 to 16.4:1. In 1963, there was an upscale version of the 750 called the DAFfodil Type 30, followed by the 31 and 32, that featured some styling changes, including a revised front end and a more heavily chromed grill. The series lived on as the Model 33 after 1967 with minor mechanical and styling changes and was in production as late as 1974. The series started with the two-door sedan and pickup and was joined later by a van and a combi, a van with rear side windows. DAFs were imported into the United States between 1959-65 in limited number. Some 33,632 DAF 750 and DAFfodil 30s were built. Production numbers of Type 31s, 32s, and 33s were 75,306, 41,255, and 131,618, respectively, including pickups, vans, and combis.

1966-76 DAF Type 44, 46, 55, and 66, and Volvo 66

The Model 44 had an 844cc, 40hp engine. When a single-belt version of the Variomatic was used after 1974, the Model 44 became the Model 46, which also got a de Dion rear suspension setup. The Type 44 was DAF's most popular model with 167,902 built between 1966 and 1974. Another 25,365 Type 46s were produced.

The DAF 55 represented a major change as a Renault-built 1108cc, four-cylinder, water-cooled, 54hp engine was used. Model 55 included a coupe; the upscale version of this was the "Marathon," to honor a DAF success in the London-to-Sydney Marathon Rally. There were 164,230 DAF 55s produced between 1967 and 1972. A two-door station wagon, called an Estate, was available in the DAF 44, 46, 55, and 66 series.

The DAF 66 appeared in 1972 to replace the DAF 55. It had a new body and the 1108cc Renault engine. A 1298cc Renault-built four-cylinder rated at 57hp was eventually available as an option in the Marathon. For ultimate performance, there was a turbocharged version of the 1289cc engine with 95hp, giving the DAF 66 Turbo Coupe a top speed of over 110mph. DAF built 138,733 DAF 66s between 1972 and 1975.

In 1975, Volvo took over DAF, and the DAF 66 became the Volvo 66. It was sold through 1978. It was then replaced by the

THE NAKED DAF
DAF 33 Ghost View

With Variomatic, power is transmitted from the engine to the rear wheels via an automatic, two-stage, centrifugal clutch attached to the engine's flywheel, two pairs of pulleys with movable flanges, and two V-belts, one for each wheel. Centrifugal weights on the front-driving pulleys, with assistance from an engine vacuum controlled by the throttle position, force the flanges on the pulley to move closer together as the car travels faster, allowing the engine to operate at essentially the same rpm. This effectively increases the diameter of the front pulley. At the same time, the flanges on the rear-driven pulley are pulled apart against spring pressure by the tension of the belt, so the effective diameter of the rear pulley is decreased. The end result is a decreasing gear ratio as vehicle speed increases. *DAF Club of America*

The first Saab, the 1950 Saab 92. With great aerodynamics, it could be pushed to just over 60mph. Until 1953, green was the only color available. *Saab-Scania AB*

Volvo 300 series, which offered the CVT transmission through 1991, but now as an option to a normal five-speed.

Saab

Svenska Aeroplan AB was founded in 1937 to build military aircraft. After World War II, it needed to diversify as orders for military aircraft were drying up. Auto building was chosen as a logical industry to use Saab's aircraft designing and manufacturing capability. The first 92001 prototype in 1946 was an unconventional car. The radial styling resulted in a drag coefficient of only 0.32 that is still admired today. Unit body

'50-56 92 2-door sedan	★★★★
'56-60 93 2-door sedan	★★★
'56 94 Sonett Super Sport	★★★★★
'60-68 95 2-door station wagon	★★★
'61-68 96 2-door sedan	★★
'58-62 Granturismo 750	★★★★
'62-67 Granturismo 850	★★★
'66-67 Sonett II 2-door coupe	★★★★

The Saab 93B in 1958 got a one-piece windshield. The suicide front doors were replaced in 1960 on the 93F. *Saab-Scania AB*

construction was used. The 92001 mechanics were heavily influenced by the postwar DKW, including front-wheel drive and a two-stroke, two-cylinder engine. The 92001 was far from a beauty, so Saab artist-designer Sixten Sason was charged with improving its looks. The result was the 92002 with the basic shape seen on Saabs right through the 1970s.

1950-56 Saab 92

By 1949, Saabs were in production. They were powered by a two-stroke, two-cylinder engine that produced 25hp at 3800rpm from 764cc. Specs included four-wheel, torsion-bar, independent suspension, a three-speed, steering-column-shifted transmission, and thermosyphon cooling. Besides more colors, 1953 brought a trunk lid and bigger rear windows. By 1954, power was upped to 28hp and a bit of chrome was added. Around 20,000 Saab 92s were built.

1956-60 Saab 93

While the 93 shared the 92's basic body and chassis, it was a different car. The engine had an additional cylinder and was now mounted transversely, but still two-cycle. Horsepower was up to 33 from 748cc. There was a new transmission which was still column shifted. A fan, thermostat, and water pump replaced the thermosyphon circulation system. The body was restyled with new fenders, grille, and hood. In a step backwards, the Saab 93 used a rigid rear suspension setup with coil springs. The wheelbase was increased from 97in to 98in. There was a new instrument panel. A total of 52,731 Saab 93s were built between 1955 and 1960. The first shipment of Saab 93s reached the United States in late 1956.

1956 Saab 94 (Sonett Super Sport)

The Sonett was designed for competition and as a concept car to display features that would show up in later Saabs. Underneath the fiberglass body were Saab 93 mechanics and a new floor pan constructed of riveted aluminum using monocoque construction around box sections. The Super Sports weighed a mere 1,100lb and had a height of only 32.5in. Overall length was a short 138in. The lines were exceedingly simple with huge wheel cutouts for the 15in wheels. The two-stroke, three-cylinder, 748cc powerplant from the 93 was tweaked to obtain 57hp. It had a top speed of over 100mph.

1958-62 Granturismo 750

Few besides Saab have mass produced

Only a half-dozen Saab 94 Sonett Super Sports were built. With its plexiglass wraparound windshield and lack of side windows, it was rather unsuited to Swedish weather. When Sixten Saxton, the car's designer, saw the finished product he declared "Sa natt den ar," or, "So neat it is." When the first two Swedish words were anglicized, it came out sounding like "so-net." *Saab-Scania AB*

From the outside, about the only difference between the rally-ready Granturismo 750 and the Saab 93 were the twin chrome side rub strips, the "SAAB GRANTURISMO 750" markings, and chrome road lights up front. *Saab-Scania AB*

While no larger than the Saab 93 and 96, the Saab 95 station wagons could carry seven with two sitting on a rearward facing seat. *Saab-Scania AB*

cars especially for rallying, a popular motorsport in Sweden. The three-cylinder engine put out 45hp and was achieved by a higher compression ratio (9.8 versus 7.3:1), polished inlet and exhaust ports, modified exhaust, twin Solex carburetion, and twin fuel pumps. More power was available, up to 57hp in the GT 750 Super, but at the expense of daily drivability, for this version was strictly for competition. Standard equipment on the GT 750 included a wood and aluminum steering wheel, sports car tires, a tachometer, a Halda Speedpilot, and world-acclaimed seats for the people up front. In the rear there were only 2+2 accommodations. It was not until 1960 that a four-speed was fitted; it was still column shifted. And while the rest of the Saabs were fitted with the 841cc engine in 1960, the GT 750 retained the 748cc engine, which now produced 50hp compared to 841's 38. The 748cc allowed the GT 750 to remain competitive in the under-750cc class. While the GT 750 was offered until 1962, it did get the updated Model 96 body in 1960.

1962-68 Saab Sport, Granturismo 850, and Monte Carlo 850

With the GT 850, known as the Saab Sport overseas, you got front disc brakes and either Pirelli Cinturato or Dunlop SP tires. The 1962 GT 850 was the first Saab to have front disc brakes, and Saab was one of the first auto makers to offer dual diagonal

braking, which came in 1964. Initially, the 841cc engine was rated at 52hp and featured three Solex carburetors, a compression ratio of 9:1, and separate lubrication. Three more horsepower came in 1965, but engine tuners were able to get 80+hp out of the 841cc powerplant. In 1964, the Granturismo 850 was retitled the Monte Carlo 850 after the great rally in which the car often competed and won in 1962 and 1963. In 1967, the Ford V-4 was added to the series, and the car became the Monte Carlo V4.

1959-68 Saab 95

From 1959 through 1978, 1968 for the two-stroke engine, Saab produced a station wagon variant of the Saab, calling it the Saab 95. The design and mechanical changes through the years paralleled those found on the Saab 93 and 96 sedans. However, the 1959 Saab 95 did have the 38hp engine that would appear on the 1960 Saab and a four-speed transmission that would not be used on the sedans for a few more years. The airfoil added on the Saab 95 after 1961 helped keep the rear window clean. Saab built 110,527 station wagons in two decades of production.

1961-68 Saab 96

The second major facelift to the Saab occurred with the Saab 96, and engine displacement was increased to 841cc with a horsepower rating of 38. In 1965, the Saab 96 was given a completely new front end treatment, the one it would retain through the 1970s with only changes in trim, headlights,

Changes for the Saab 96 included new rear fenders, much larger rear window, and a larger luggage compartment. *Bill Siuru*

The Saab Sonett II's chassis components were the same as those used on the Saab 96, but the wheelbase was shortened to 85in. *Bill Siuru*

and bumpers. In 1965, the radiator was moved from behind the engine to up in front of the engine. The engine produced 40hp in 1965. In 1966, triple carburetors were added and power was boosted to 42hp. A four-speed, column-shifted transmission was now standard. For the performance oriented, there was the Saab 96 Special with a 55hp engine and front disc brakes. After 1967, all Saabs had front disc brakes.

The Saab 96 would continue in production through 1979, although in latter years they were not exported to the United States. The biggest change in Saab's history occurred in 1967, a four-stroke, V-4 engine! The Ford-built, 1498cc V-4 was used in the 96 after 1967. Saab did not completely abandon two-strokes until after 1968. For the U.S. market, Saab reduced the displacement of the two-stroke to 816cc (49.8cid), calling it the Shrike, and offering it only in 1968 but with the older 1967 style body. With less than 50cid, it could pass U.S. emission requirements.

The end of the model run in 1979 represented three-decades of Saab's use of the same basic design. Of course, there were constant design and engineering changes. A total of 547,221 Saab 96s were built.

1966-74 Sonett II, Sonett V4, and Sonett III

Saab mass produced only one two-seater sports car, the Sonett series. This is by far the most collectable, readily available Saab. The rarest of the production Sonetts are the 258 1966 and 1967 Sonett IIs powered by three-cylinder, two-stroke, 60hp, 841cc engines, including the rather unsportscar-like column-mounted gear selector. The Sonett's pretty body was designed by Bjorn Karlstrom and was made of fiberglass. With a drag coefficient of 0.32, this was a 100mph car. The Sonetts came with a proper roll bar behind the seat to support the fiberglass roof, especially in a roll-over accident. In 1967, the Saab sports car also got the Ford 1498cc, V-4 engine, and the two-stroke version was discontinued.

Index